To

Gill Fielding

It Is My Life
And I'm In Charge

Take Charge of Your Life

xoxo

felicity Okolo

It Is My Life
And I'm In Charge

Felicity Okolo
Dynamic Life Coach & Speaker

http://www.felicityokolo.com

London

Email: felicity@felicityokolo.com

ISBN 978-1-4507-5148-3

This book is dedicated to my three children:
Jubilant, Claire and Louis-Marie who were my
reason for hanging onto life through the
adversity described in this book.

I feel blessed and privileged to be
their mother. I love you all.

Acknowledgments

I dreamed the 'impossible' dream of empowering millions of women. I conceived a powerful title and was given the right support team to make this dream come true for which I am humbly and deeply thankful and eternally appreciative.

My sincere gratitude goes to Andrew Priestly and Elena Borissova for making me see how I can transform and save lives of women who have experienced domestic violence and make other women aware of this plague. They ignited the fire that made this book possible. Also Raja Hireker for his encouragement in making sure I stay focused on target.

I love and thank my husband Ugochukwu Benjamin Onyebalu who supported and comforted me when I broke down several times while writing the book due to the sheer horror of what I had experienced. I deeply appreciate him for his love, understanding and encouragement.

I love and thank my children: Jubilant, Claire and Louis-Marie for supporting me and offering their permission to share this story with the world. I deeply appreciate their love, understanding and encouragement.

I thank, respect and appreciate my editor and proof reader Jill McKellan for making sure this book is perfect and ready for you to read.

I thank, respect and appreciate my designer Rosamond Grupp for giving this book the beautiful and powerful touch it has.

I thank, respect, appreciate and love my friend Richie Dayo Johnson for his support and encouragement while this book is being conceived and during the writing process.

My special thanks goes to my mastermind group members: Frank Lee, Joni Dunn, Vanessa Pacheco, Shelley Osterried and Sussana Huse for their encouragement and love.

I am so blessed to call her my Auntie and mum right from the moment I arrived in the UK till this day. Her unending and untiring support, love and encouragement leave me speechless. Her support and love when I broke down several times recalling horrible memories and encouragement when I wanted to give up writing this book just shows how much love she has for me. All I can say here is God bless you and thank you to Kate Ego Ugochukwu.

Wow! How did I get so blessed to have dad, mum and sisters all wrapped in one family who saved me, helped and supported my children and me throughout my adversity and beyond. Words cannot express my gratitude to them and neither can gifts say how grateful I am to Tom Snow, Helen Penn, Loveday Penn-Kekana, Clemency Rachel Penn and Eleanor Beanie Snow. I thank you all for your lifelong help and love.

My biggest thanks go to the Author of Life Himself-God. Thank You for your wisdom. Thank you for my courage and strength during that period, now and forever.

XOXO

Contents

There is no education like adversity.

– Benjamin Disraeli

Who Will Benefit From This Book?

Everybody Will Benefit From This Book!
Determine Your Needs And Promote Awareness

If you are in a hurry and just want to learn the steps to eradicate domestic violence you should read the introduction and conclusion.

If you want to understand why that eradication method is vital then read the introduction, my take on domestic violence and conclusion.

If you want a summary of tactics abusers use and the critical, yet effective strategies I have used to be a survivor – not a statistic – read the introduction, lessons at end of each chapter, and the conclusion.

If you want to learn strategies I used to survive and conquer domestic violence so you can fully understand why domestic violence is a plague that affects every person on a global level, then read the entire book.

If you want informative resources and training on domestic violence issues or concerns, visit:

www.felicityokolo.com

or email: felicity@felicityokolo.com

If you agree that domestic abuse and violence must be eradicated you agree that this book is a **must have**. It will give you the information you need to promote awareness, prevention, and the ultimate goal – eradication!

Introduction

You've most likely heard or read other women's survival stories of domestic violence. My story of domestic violence may not be so different, but what you will discover in this book has the potential to help you, your loved ones, friends or neighbours begin to recognise, cope, survive and conquer domestic violence.

Domestic violence is called by many names.
It is referred to as:

- domestic abuse

- battering

- intimate partner violence

No matter what name you give this ugly violence you must know this one thing, *"It is a pattern of controlling and aggressive behaviours from one adult towards another within the context of an intimate relationship."*

It can be physical, sexual, psychological or emotional abuse. Financial abuse and social isolation are also common traits that can be found within domestic violence.

My success in eradicating domestic violence from my life brought me to two things that I am very passionate about; being a Life Coach and professional Transformational Speaker. I have seen so many professional women who still suffer domestic violence. As a professional woman, I believe – I know – that it is wrong to hear that these horrors are still happening to women across the world. Many people assume that professional women cannot fall victim to these ruthless acts, but that is not true. It is so sad and I am committed to being the voice that brings awareness and my ultimate goal – eradication of domestic violence.

The purpose of this book is to share my own experience and the strategies I used to cope, survive and conquer domestic violence when all odds seemed to be stacked against me.

Domestic violence ignores all limitations. It is no respecter of age, race, culture, religion or position. In the **United Kingdom, two women a week are killed** by a current or former male partner. One in four women will experience domestic violence in their lifetime – many of these on a number of occasions. One incident of domestic violence is reported to the police every minute. These statistics are in accordance with the findings of the Women's Aid Charity. In the United States, one in four women will experience domestic violence in their lifetime according to National Coalition Against Domestic Violence (NCADV). According to the U.S. Department of Justice's National Crime Victimization Survey (NCVS), a domestic violence act occurs every 15 seconds in the United States resulting in about 2.5

million women experiencing domestic violence each year. On average, **three women are killed every day in the U.S** due to domestic violence according to The National Organization for Women.

I don't view my story as just another sad tale that fortunately had a happy ending. It is a story that was given to me to share with others. Every woman needs to know this one thing: even when all odds are stacked against you, you can rise above them and become extremely successful if you choose. How do you make your choice? You make it based on your level of awareness. I wish one thing for women everywhere: I hope they become more aware of available strategies and resources to make choices that take them out of their violent situations.

It is my hope that you, the reader, will learn from my mistakes and especially from my courage to survive without remaining a victim. The difference between me and the women who didn't survive is that I became aware of my choices and acted on them.

To download a FREE eBook on surviving domestic violence please visit:

www.survivingdomesticviolence.info

or send an email to:

felicity@felicityokolo.com.

I will send you a copy of the eBook that will take you from victim to a woman of courage who made the choice to stop the violence and reclaim her true purpose.

There is one other thing that I wish for you, the reader. I hope you learn how to become fearless and trust your intuition. You must know and believe that surviving domestic violence is possible and conquering it is even a greater achievement. When you overcome and conquer domestic violence, you come to take charge of your life and live the happy, loving life that you so deserve. That becomes your belief and it doesn't matter what anybody else thinks because they have no power over your happiness any longer.

Your life is in your hands. Only you can make it what you want it to be. Many women have been through what you are going through. Some, like me, are lucky to be alive, but others have become the unlucky ones. You don't need luck – you need a choice. That's what this book is about – hope. After all, you need to reclaim yourself and say, **"IT IS MY LIFE AND I'M IN CHARGE."**

Help is available for you online or offline at Citizens Advice Bureaux. If you are unsure of what to do call **999 if in the UK and 911 if in the US** and the police will help and guide you to the right services.

Read on.

PART ONE

Do not fear the winds of adversity. Remember: A kite rises against the wind rather than with it.

– Unknown Author

CHAPTER ONE

In The Beginning

It was a fall afternoon, October 1989 to be specific. I was in Maiduguri, Borno State, Nigeria, when I shared a taxi with my secondary school Home Economics/Food & Nutrition teacher. That is where my story starts. Within five short months I was married to her brother in London, England. This story will be told from beginning to end – just as it happened. I invite you to share this journey with me. It is a journey that helped me discover amazing things that I never knew I had in me. It took all my collective childhood learning from my mother (my rock, my foundation); plus my spiritual learning and sheer wisdom from God to get through the things that happened to me.

We boarded the taxi from University of Maiduguri Campus where I was studying foundation in Laboratory Technology. The progression was to lead to a degree in Microbiology. I was going to the Nigerian Television Authority (NTA) for a rehearsal for a TV drama show I was a part of. When I got to my stop, I paid my fare and that of my ex-teacher. She then said to me, "Oh, I just remembered, I had you in mind a while ago, but could not contact you. There is something very important I would like to discuss with you." She wrote her address onto a piece of paper and gave it to me. We agreed on a date and the taxi drove off. At the time, I didn't think much more about it since I was so busy.

It had been three years since I saw my former teacher. I wondered what was so important that she wanted to speak with me. When I arrived at her address, she welcomed me and offered me a drink. After exchanging pleasantries, she revealed what she wanted to discuss with me. She told me her elder brother in London, England, wanted a wife. From his specifications I was the ideal person for him. She said he wanted a well-behaved girl from a good family. She needed to be intelligent, have a fair complexion, an athletic build and be tall. I was all of those things. She wanted to take a picture of me to send to him. After he received it the discussion could continue from there. I could not believe what I just heard. In fact, I was astonished. "I am not sure if I'm interested in this proposal" I said to her. We left it at that. She went on to say that she knew my father and would approach him directly about the matter.

I left her house feeling confused and afraid. I was 19 and in love – not with her brother in England, but with someone else in the University. I returned to my college campus and told my boyfriend, whom I shall call Jim, about the visit. He said what I told him just confirmed the fear he had when I first told him about the woman's request to visit her at home. He was worried and shocked. He told me how he hadn't been aware that it was part of my culture for parents to arrange marriages for their daughters. He knew those practices were common in Northern Nigeria, where he was from, but didn't know they also were considered in Eastern Nigeria.

My ex-teacher proceeded to visit my parents. She informed them of her mission to find a wife for her brother per his instructions. My parents requested I come home one weekend for a meeting about the matter. During the meeting I told them I was not interested in marrying someone I didn't know regardless of where he was from or what he had. Besides, I was not old enough to get married. They persuaded me to send my photo and said that he may have found someone else or may not be interested in me. Just to get them off my case, I pulled out a photo from my album and sent it to my ex-teacher. She, in turn, sent it off to her brother.

I received a beautiful postcard directly from my "would-be" husband. Next, there was a letter saying he would like to marry me and would be coming to Nigeria to make the arrangements. It was only four months since I had shared a taxi with my ex-teacher and now I was about to marry her brother? I was in disbelief and really couldn't accept it. I never even liked the woman when she was my teacher. No one in school liked her. She was very mean, strict and aggressive; plus she hardly smiled. I was simply being polite when I paid her taxi fare that day. I knew she had liked me when she was my teacher, despite my indifference to her.

However, I just didn't care for her. It was probably just the subject she taught. I had to take it and didn't care for it at all. Now, this old teacher was somehow involved in my life more deeply than I would have ever thought possible.

My "would-be" husband arrived in Nigeria just a few weeks after getting my letter, much to my surprise. I was asked to go and meet him at the hotel where he was staying. I went to see him and did not know what to think of him. Up to that point, all I wanted in and of a man was someone who loved me madly and was God-fearing. When evening came I wanted to return to my college but he insisted I spend the night. I was a little afraid and did not have a change of clothing. Despite my intuition, I complied rather than make a scene. I wanted to sleep on the floor but he insisted I sleep on the bed.

That night I shared a bed with the stranger. My clothes were tightly wrapped around me. I didn't want to get under the covers with him because he was half naked. The air conditioner was cranked up high and eventually I got too cold and slid under the covers. I pretended to sleep. I felt his hands reach over to touch me. He was trying to undress me and wasn't fazed that I was supposedly asleep. I quickly slapped his hand off me. I jumped out of the bed and was set to leave when he said that he just wanted to get to know me better.

I told him in no uncertain terms that I hardly knew him and went on to ask, "Is this your way of getting to know me better, by wanting to have sex with me?" I told him we were not even married. I thought that if I had any control over the situation we'd never be married.

He apologised and asked me to come back to bed. I listened to his command and definitely didn't even doze off for the rest of the night. I lay in that bed and prayed to God to keep me safe and patiently waited for the light of morning to come. It couldn't get there quick enough.

As soon as the light started to show through the hotel room window I snuck out of the hotel room. I hadn't brushed my teeth and my clothes were wrinkled. I felt so disgusting and I had done nothing wrong.

I was very upset and hated the man for wanting to have sex with me before marriage. I went back to my college housing to shower, change and go see my parents. They needed to hear my feedback of this vile man.

Once I was safely at my parent's home, I told them how he had wanted to have sex with me and this upset my father. I told them again I did not want to marry the man because for all we knew he could be lying about who he is and why he was in London. He claimed to be an accountant with a home of his own and tenants. He'd promised me a life of comfort and all I had to do in exchange was collect the rents, help him, go to college and live happily ever. He had prepared for everything. Still, despite his grand words, I didn't trust him.

In the end, my parents chose to ignore my fears and concerns. They believed this man and trusted his sister. A long time back, my father and his sister attended a teacher training institution together. She knew that she had earned the like and trust of my father through that experience. That, combined with being my ex-teacher at the college where my father was in charge of admissions, was enough to convince my parents that I was just being overly sensitive.

The entire situation just seemed too convenient to me. I felt I was fighting a losing battle because the promise of a better life for me seemed glamorous to my parents. Plus, it will be one less child for them to look after. I was the second of seven children from a working class family. I thought my parents almost appeared desperate to have one less 'burden' lifted from their shoulders. They went ahead and scheduled the marriage date.

On the day of the marriage ceremony I refused to go home. My parents sent me a message through a friend of mine who lived opposite of me at home and was in same University as me. They wanted me to come home for the ceremony, but I refused. I was in Jim's college room with Jim and so confused. I poured out tears that were filled with deep grief. I sent my college friend away to say I wouldn't go and I was not going to marry that man. My college friend was sent back to tell me that if I did not come home I should no longer consider them my parents. Outside the college, there was a taxi waiting to take me back home. After about an hour of continuous tears and clinging to Jim, my college friend finally persuaded me that it would be best to go and also, I couldn't isolate myself from my family.

I finally agreed because of a backup plan I made with Jim. The plan was to go marry the stranger just to please my parents and then I would leave him. I was scared of eloping with Jim, whom I truly loved, because I was very close with my mum and I didn't want to cause her heartache by just disappearing. I would miss her way too much to do something like that.

I was armed with a plan that I was not sure how to execute. Still, I boarded the taxi with tears freely flowing and headed off towards my home. A new husband and ceremony were there waiting for the miserable bride.

As I pulled up to my parents' house, I saw my future husband, a man 16 years my senior, waiting for me. He looked genuinely excited and I looked like a big puffer fish. My eyes were swollen from crying. I could not look at him. I hated him; his sister and my parents for making me do what I did not want to do. They put Jim and me under so much stress. They were denying us the opportunity for true happiness and love just to fulfil a selfish wish.

My parents had invited a handful of family and friends. He just had his sister and her husband. They had no other people present. In a flash the ceremony was over. Then I learned I had to go to my now husband's place after that. I had thought I would at least have some time with my family, but that was not how it was done. I just had to go and live with him. Now, I was all alone and married to a stranger whom I despised. He had no house or place for us to go back to. Instead, we went back to his sister's house, where a room had already being prepared for the bride and groom. Yippee!

During the drive back to his sister's house I kept thinking and praying that my parents would be right for believing in this man. If his sister was nice, he would be nice and the good life he had promised would be true. I went along with the fact that my parents had my best interests at heart. I had always dreamed of living abroad and having a glamorous lifestyle. Maybe they saw this as my opportunity to fulfil my dreams.

My parents and his sister had expressed to me that people have had marriages arranged before. It wasn't so bad and all you needed to do is grow to love the other. The only place I had seen forced and arranged marriages was in Indian movies. That was a movie – not something that would ever happen to me. Wrong! I have also known girls as young as 14 getting married in Nigeria. I assumed that they expected to get married that young as part of their culture, but I had never imagined I would experience it personally.

We arrived at his sister's house and I was shown the prepared room. All I wanted to do was sleep. I was exhausted from crying so much that day. Besides, I hoped I would wake up to find it was all a bad dream. That night, as tradition would have it, I had to fulfil my marital duties by having sex with him. It was awful. I hated it and I hated him especially as he kept calling me 'Christine', someone else's name. This went on for a couple of nights. He even called me that name during the day sometimes. I wanted to know who 'Christine' was. When I asked him he actually denied it and told me that I must have heard wrong. I asked his sister and she said 'Christine' was a cousin of theirs that he was fond of. She went on to say that 'Christine' looked like me and that's why her brother was getting the names mixed up. For some reason I let it go even though it did not make sense. You could see the awkwardness in his sister's body language when she explained who 'Christine' was. She didn't want to talk about it, yet I decided just to let it go.

New rules were laid out for me. My now husband, whom I shall call Simon, told me he had learned of the boyfriend I had at the university. I was forbidden from having any contact with him. He went on to say that anyone who wants to see me must visit me in his sister's house. He also instructed me to stop any contraceptive I may be using right away.

He had bought some outfits to give to me. I thought they could have been for anyone, but they were now mine. Some fitted but I had to give some away because they were too small. Just a few days later I had to go to the university campus to collect my belongings. That was the end of college for me.

Saying Goodbye To My Boyfriend Jim

I arrived at the university and was surprised to find I was the gossip of the campus. I ignored the gossips and told a handful of people the summary of events. I gathered my things together before going to see Jim, probably for the last time. Jim looked different. He could hardly speak to me. All he could do was cry. I cried with him and comforted him. I told him I would be leaving in a week or so and that I wasn't sure how our plan would work out. I promised to write to him in secret and then we would take it from there. I promised to always love him and he promised to always love me too.

A week later, Simon and I set off to the British High Commission in Kaduna State Nigeria, to get my visa before leaving for London. I said my farewell to my family and off we went.

It didn't go well at the British High Commission and my visa application was refused. I was disappointed, but he was even more disappointed. When I asked him why, he mumbled something that I did not understand and he would not repeat it. He started an appeal against the High Commissions decision. He brought me back to his sister's house in Maiduguri, completed the appeal form, and said he would send me money to go back to Kaduna to submit the appeal because he'd be returning to England in just a few days.

Just a couple of weeks after he left, as I was planning to go back to Kaduna State to submit the appeal form, I became sick. I was vomiting so my sister-in-law took me to a clinic. It turned out I was pregnant. My mind swirled with chaos. What was I going to do? What about the plan with Jim? There was no mention of pregnancy in the plan. I was confused and felt seriously trapped. I also felt shame for four main reasons:

1. I was a catholic girl who had not yet been wed in the church and I was pregnant.

2. I was well known in the city because of my TV show and had bid farewell to everyone.

3. I could not face people being pregnant from a man who was not around.

4. I didn't know how I could face Jim?
   What would he say? What would he
   think of me?

The trip to England for my new life was postponed until
I felt better. By now my sister-in-law was the boss of me.
She dictated where I went and when I went there. She told
me who I saw and for what reasons. She even told me the
right time to change my toothbrush. The toothbrush lecture
was the last straw. Simon had sent me money and she was
keeping it for me. I wanted a new toothbrush and she refused
to buy me one. I explained to her that I change toothbrush
every month and it was time for a new one. She said there
was no need to change toothbrush every month. This made
me mad and it was a good opportunity to take out my frus-
tration on her. I cried and yelled at her; demanding all the
money Simon sent for me. I told her I was capable of look-
ing after my money and myself. I threatened she had better
give me what I wanted or I would return to my parents. She
called Simon and he made her give me all my money. Simon
was very pleased to hear about the pregnancy and promised
that in no time I would soon join him in England.

* * *

About two weeks after I discovered I was pregnant, I at-
tended mass in a catholic church close to my sister-in-law's
house. After mass, someone told me a man was asking for
me outside the church. It was Jim. He was patiently waiting
for me that day. I was surprised, but pleased. At first I could
not recognise him because he had lost so much weight. He

looked as if he was becoming anorexic. He had not been eating or sleeping properly since I left and I feared how he would cope with his final exams just a month away. I reached out and hugged him. He was cold towards me. I told him that it was too risky for him to come and see me. He said he didn't care. He wanted to see me because he knew I was pregnant. When I asked how he knew, he replied that he'd dreamt about it. He said he wanted to know if the pregnancy was his. Before I could answer, he went on to say he would do whatever it takes to claim his baby, even if that meant preventing me from leaving the country. I told him the baby was not his, even though deep in my heart I wanted it to be his. I told him I had a period after I got married, so the baby could not be his. He was disappointed.

We stood outside the church that day; everyone else had left. We didn't have much to say and I was getting worried that my sister-in-law would start wondering why I'd been gone so long. I didn't want her to come looking for me. We just looked at each other with broken hearts and tears running down our cheeks. It was hard to say goodbye again. For the very last time, we hugged, stole a kiss and I didn't want to let go of the only loving embrace I had ever known from a man. He held me ever so tightly. I had to pull away and told him that my sister-in-law may not let me go to church anymore if she suspected I met him there.

I blew Jim, my love, a kiss and said goodbye. He stood there and watched me walk away. Tears streamed down my face and I had never felt so miserable and alone. That day, in front of the church, was the last time I saw Jim.

The Deception

I was married for five months and still in Nigeria. I took a trip every month since Simon left to Kaduna to apply for a visa to join him. We were dissuaded from appealing and thus a new application was made. The same decision came back and I was still refused a visa. There was no reason given to me. On the fifth occasion I demanded a reason. I let them know I was pregnant travelling on rough roads with large potholes to try and get to my husband. I wanted to know why I had to keep going through this process with no explanation. I was always amazed that the baby didn't seem disturbed by the journey. My body, on the other hand, suffered from it greatly.

The lady who interviewed me on this occasion asked me to find out why I was refused a visa from Simon because he knew why. I went back to Maiduguri, called Simon and told him what the lady at the High Commission said. He promised to come the following month.

Six months had gone by since my marriage. I found that I was a pregnant, frustrated, married woman living with a woman who annoyed me and no closer to knowing my husband than I was on the first day we met. My sister-in-law said we should start buying baby things in Nigeria, but I did not like that plan. Simon came back to Nigeria and for the sixth time I went to the British High Commission for a Visa with Simon. This time Simon presented a new document before my visa was granted to join him for six months. I asked him what the document that he presented to the High Commission was and he said it was a divorce certificate. I could not believe what I heard. I was so upset. I asked him why he kept asking me to go for visa interviews when he knew that I would not be granted visa because he was still legally married to someone else. He just said that he didn't think it would have made a difference. He got that one right – he didn't think.

The delay in getting my visa was a sign of deception that I did not like. Simon finally revealed that his ex-wife's name was 'Christine' the name he used to call me when we first got married. Things were making sense now and I was starting to get scared, especially since I was about to leave the country. I asked him if he had told my parents that he was married and he said no. I could not believe that he and his sister lied to both my parents and I. I was very trusting; I guess my parents were very trusting as well. This was not a good start. My fears were coming true and this was just the beginning. What else could he be hiding? What would happen to me when I got to England with him I wondered? Even with all the thoughts exploding in my mind I still felt a sense of relief for my baby. I was glad that I would not be having my baby in Nigeria without its father. I would also be able to stop the shame I felt when people believed that Simon had abandoned me. We left Nigeria two days later and headed for the UK.

Do not bite at the bait of pleasure,
till you know there is no hook
beneath it.

– Thomas Jefferson

CHAPTER LESSONS

Abusers Controlling Tactics

1. Lies and cover-ups.
2. False promises.
3. Exploitation of my circumstances with promise of financial security.
4. Entered into the relationship for selfish gains.

My Strategies

1. Naivety by believing things would get better.

Could Have Done & Recommendations

1. Check spouse/partner out to find out if there was violence in his family.
2. Marry a spouse for LOVE only. Anything else is not worth it.
3. Discuss your 'ideal' happy, loving relationship with your partner and listen to your partners 'ideals' as well. Do this before getting married or settling with a partner.
4. Discuss your views about domestic violence firmly and with love. Tell your future partner you will not tolerate it and if you see any sign of it you will leave.
5. Refuse to marry him.

CHAPTER TWO

Coming To England

I arrived in England and was equally shocked and awed by the autumn weather. I wrote to my parents describing all the new and 'better' things in England. Maybe this might just work out after all and I would get the lifestyle I always dreamed of in England. I did not tell them about Simon's ex-wife. I don't remember why. Maybe I didn't want them to be worried, perhaps I didn't want to admit it myself, or possibly I didn't think it was important because it was in the past and done. I also wrote to Jim telling him how I missed him. I promised him that once I had the baby we would start working on our plan.

Three and half months later, I gave birth to my first baby. That winter I saw both my beautiful baby boy and snow for the first time ever. In fact, it snowed on the day I gave birth and it didn't stop for three days. I was in the hospital the entire time. On the third day we went home. Simon held the baby because I was afraid of dropping him if I slipped in the snow. I wasn't about to take any chances.

Controlling Behaviour

Soon after my son was born I got a response to my letter from Jim. He told me how much he missed me. Simon had intercepted my letter and read it before handing it to me. I could not believe he read my letter before me, especially this letter from Jim. He interrogated me about the letter. Finally he told me that Jim could not do much with me since I was so far away; unless his penis was as long as the distance from Nigeria to England.

I was hurt by Simon's invasion of my privacy and told him I did not like him reading my letters. That did not stop him. He opened and read all mail that came for me. So I wrote to Jim telling him that it was not a good idea to keep writing me. I explained how Simon was reading all my mail and it might cause problems for us. I didn't want our plan to be jeopardised. That letter that Simon intercepted was the first and only letter I got from Jim. I cherished it so much and would read it over and over. It was my comfort and solace when Simon would try to harm me with his spiteful, mean words.

I had been in England, a strange country, for only four months with a new baby. I had no friends or family. My husband was a stranger who controlled me and censored all my letters and called me vile names. Plus, I had not been going to church so I began to feel as though I was losing my spiritual connection with God.

The nearest Catholic Church was two bus rides away and I couldn't drive. Simon worked on Sundays or Saturday nights and claimed he was too tired to drive me to church. I kept asking him to drive me but Simon kept refusing. Since the baby was born I began to miss church increasingly more. This made me anxious because I wanted the baby to be christened and Thanksgiving was important too. I kept persisting that Simon should take me and reminded him of his commitments he'd made to my parents and I back in Nigeria. He had promised to take me to church because he knew I was very religious. I also reminded him that he promised my parents and I that we would be wed in the Catholic Church as soon as I give birth and we would raise our children as Catholics. Simon had assured me that I could take the children to any church I wanted and he didn't mind because he didn't have time for church.

In the end, Simon was not interested in the baby's christening or Thanksgiving. He certainly wasn't interested in taking me to church and finally told me so. That's when he threw in that he was a Jehovah's Witness and wanted our children to be raised the same. That meant they would have to be adults to be baptised. Simon continued with his feelings and revealed to me that he had no intention of wedding me. He only made that promise to make my parents and I happy so that the marriage would take place. He went on to say that not all promises made to a woman before marriage needed to be fulfilled.

This hurt me and I felt deceived. I was deceived, but there was more. He went on to say that he didn't even approve of me going to church. As a Jehovah's Witness he didn't even have the time to attend their meetings and that meant that I shouldn't go anywhere near my church or even consider working. He continued by saying the only friends I could have needed to be approved by him and I needed permission to see them. When I asked why, he said it was because his ex-wife was allowed to mix with other people and she got corrupted from their behaviour. She felt that she had wised up and ended up leaving him and filed for divorce. Simon saw this as a disgrace and promised himself that it would not happen to him again. Simon claimed that the divorce was the reason why he was forced to sell his property in South Wales, where he and his ex-wife lived before moving to London. They only moved to London because she requested it. Simon continued to say that the loss of his property, combined with a divorce, made him vow to never let anyone he married mix with other people. This rule especially applied to associating with Ghanaians. He was very bitter and upset as he spoke. I told him I was a different person and it hurt to be punished for someone else's wrongs. He refused to see the common sense and ignored my pleas.

* * *

Depression had begun to set in for me by now. Aside from the expected post-natal depression, which some women suffer after having a baby, I also had some senseless rules to obey. I couldn't even go to church to find reprieve and discovered that I would never be wed before the eyes of God. I became increasingly overworked, overtaxed and I was not well fed. Life had become a downward spiral.

The house Simon had claimed to have in London was a three-bed maisonette with lodgers in all the three bedrooms upstairs. We were downstairs and used the dining room as our bedroom. The baby's cot made our "bedroom" space very tight. I had to share both the kitchen and bathroom with the lodgers – who were strangers to me – and clean up after them. I found myself having to wait my turn to cook in my own kitchen and use my own bathroom. What kind of luxury is this I thought to myself? This was not what I had been promised? I could not have been more disappointed. When Simon first showed me where we were going to live he had taken a picture of the entire block where the flat was. He had claimed that he owned the entire building. A deceitful liar – that's what Simon was.

In Nigeria, it was normal for people to own large sized properties and I assumed it was the same in London, but I was wrong. As I sank further into my depression, the rules and lies surrounding my marriage did not help but rather made it worse. It seemed that Simon looked for any excuse to cause an argument. He complained about me not cleaning the house and told me I was lucky to be a landlady. Many women would die to be in my position, he would say.

Every now and then I would ask to speak to my parents and actually be granted permission. When I made those calls Simon would always be close by listening or right there in front of me. That made it impossible for me to tell them what was going on. They asked about the wedding plans and I made the excuse that the plan was on hold because I still had not settled properly. I certainly could not tell them about his ex-wife yet.

The only people I communicated with and became close to were the lodgers in our master bedroom – a newly married couple, my Auntie – a relative of a friend from Nigeria and our next-door neighbours. My health visitor who came to check on the baby and I could tell I was not well looked after. My unhappiness and depression were obvious but I could not tell her what was happening. TV and music became my escape and companion.

My baby was three months old now. I was quickly getting fed up with Simon's complaints and arguments that I was prepared to do anything to get away from him. At this time my visa was running out. I asked him what the right procedure was for extending visa and he promised he would sort it out. One evening I was watching TV – my only source of information about the outside world – when he walked in and started complaining about some small thing. He immediately changed the TV channel. I told him I was watching a show that I had looked forward to all day. He didn't care. He wanted to watch his own show. I said fine you could watch yours, I'll go upstairs to the lodgers and watch with them because I'd heard them talk about watching the same programme as me earlier that evening. I did this to avoid further argument because I just didn't want that. I took the baby and went upstairs. When the programme finished, I came back down but Simon was gone. The door to our living room was locked. I called out to him, but there was no answer. I could not believe he locked me out. He knew I had not taken my keys because I was still in the house. There was no need for me to take my keys just to go upstairs. So, I returned upstairs and stayed with the couple in the master bedroom.

Soon the baby started crying. He was wet and needed changing before going to sleep and it was past his bedtime. Simon was still not back and I was getting upset because my baby was distressed. Two hours later I heard him come back and I went downstairs and found that he was inside the living room, with the door locked. I called out and pleaded with him to let me in because the baby needed changing. He would not unlock the door. By now I was angry that he could be mean to his baby like that. I told him that if he did not open the door I would do whatever was necessary to enter the room so I could get the baby's nappy. He still ignored me. I took the crying baby, who was now soaked with urine out of his clothing back upstairs. I left him with the newlyweds and decided to force my way into the room. I got a screwdriver, took off the door handles and when I started chipping the wood around the lock Simon opened the door. He pulled me in and attacked me. He kept hitting me 'till I was on the floor. As he punched me in the head he was cussing and calling me names and saying that I came to England with everything prepared for me and all I did was destroy his possessions. I was on the floor helpless and screaming when the couple upstairs came to restrain him.

The couple eventually restrained him and I heard the woman say to him, "Do you want to kill her?" and he replied, "Yes, she came to this country not knowing how hard it is to make money and now she is destroying my property."

By this time I could not see properly and I was in so much pain I could no longer scream. I couldn't move from the floor. I felt like I had been pounded with a pestle. The couple had to help me up and took me out of the room.

I sat in the kitchen for a while and asked them to bring the baby down to me. The baby was now fast asleep. White dry tear tracks were stained all over his face. After about half an hour I regained some strength, but was still in pain. I slowly changed the baby, fed him, and laid him in his cot.

Within a few weeks of the beating I wrote to my parents and told them about the violence, his ex-wife, the lies and empty promises. My father wrote back and said that if I was not happy I should return home. My father was very upset about him beating me. I told Simon that if he beat me again I would leave him. I added that it was not an idle threat but a promise that I would keep. That was when Simon told me that my father had warned him that if he hit me the marriage would not work because I was against violence and my parents did not raise me with violence. I was appalled to hear him say that. I asked him why he did it if he was aware of what my stands were and my families as well. He could not answer.

Something within me was not truly convinced that my parents were serious about me coming home if I wasn't happy. It made me make the decision to stay and give it one more chance. Besides, what would people say about a Catholic Ibo girl leaving her husband to return to her parents? I felt I should give it another chance for my religious beliefs, my culture and my family. By this time, I still could not figure out a plan with Jim, but his only letter kept me going.

It was lonely, shallow and empty, but I kept on despite of Simon.

We lived on.

Every adversity, every failure,
every heartache carries with it the
seed of an equal or greater benefit.

– Napoleon Hill

CHAPTER LESSONS

Abuser's Controlling Tactics

1. Immigration threats.
2. Lack of privacy.
3. Social isolation from people and things that matter to you.
4. Financial control by promoting a lack of financial independence.
5. Physical, emotional, mental, and financial abuse.

My Strategies

1. Acknowledged that domestic violence is wrong and would not be tolerated.
2. Told husband to stop abusing me or the marriage will end.

Could Have Done & Recommendations

1. Called the police, report the abuse, and press charges.
2. Defended myself.
3. Make the choice to leave if I was ready to.

CHAPTER THREE

The Beginning Of The End

My bruises remained for about two weeks after the beating. I was black and blue all over my body. It took about four months for the remnant colouring of the bruise on my left cheek to return to my natural skin tone. Each time I saw it, I remembered the incident. No matter how hard I tried, I could not let it go.

A few days after the incident, Simon made an attempt to apologise for beating me. He did it because he wanted sex. He couldn't continue though because he could not bear to look at my swollen and bruised face – the one he was responsible for.

My health visitor knew something was wrong but I still could not tell her. Like most women, I told her the infamous lie. I'd say things like, "I walked into the door." The lies didn't stop the depression and unhappiness though. I believe she was concerned, not just for me, but more so for the baby. She was put into a situation where she had to discuss my case with the doctors, nurses and health visitors at my local

GP (general practitioner) surgery. I did not know about this at the time.

After this first physical violence incident, I knew it was the beginning of the end. I definitely did not want to raise my children in a violent home. It was just not acceptable and I couldn't tolerate it – it was wrong. I was not sure what to do or how to go about it since I was only in London for just over six months at that time. I didn't understand the laws and how these situations worked. All I knew is that violence was wrong and would not be accepted or tolerated by me.

I kept praying that the incident would never happen again. That hope was the only thing that kept me going. I started to sing to gospel music when I was alone. It lifted me up. I also sang and danced to pop and R & B when Simon wasn't there. TV was my best friend and I watched a lot of Oprah. I couldn't believe the problems people experienced until I watched an episode about domestic violence. I had no idea that domestic violence took place in other parts of the world. I thought it was an ugliness that was isolated to third world countries. This was truly a revelation for me – especially when they mentioned that the law could help women and all women were encouraged to report any violence at home.

That Oprah episode triggered a powerful memory. When I had told Simon that I will not tolerate violence and will do whatever was necessary to stop him from hitting me, he bragged. He told me that even if I called the police they would not do anything to him because there was no law against domestic violence. He added that British law had no effect in his house. I had a moment of awareness and was embarrassed at my stupidity for believing him. After all, where was this house I lived in located? How could British law not have an effect on a house on British soil? The scary part was that I wasn't sure if Simon was delusional or just a liar. It was a terrifying thought.

I had no money and was not allowed to work. He claimed that he did not want me to do menial jobs. Simon would say he wanted me to get a degree first, after which I could get a good job, yet I wasn't allowed to go to college either. Without money of my own I was not able to buy things I wanted, when I wanted them. Simon bought the food. It was always the same – turkey wings and thighs – they were the cheapest meat and could be used for soups, stews and other dishes. I was so sick of turkey as everything else. I couldn't stand turkey anymore. I couldn't taste it anymore. This put me off turkey and to this day I can only bear to eat turkey once a year at Christmas. Any other time I see turkey, I feel like vomiting.

My first baby was six months old when my Health Visitor tried to help with my isolation. I had already told her that Simon did not want me to mix with people because of his previous experience with his ex-wife. My Health Visitor thought that having another new mother to befriend would do me good because I would have someone else to share the joys and concerns about being a new parent. I was missing out on that and it was important, she said.

My Health Visitor told me about a lady who lived a few houses away from me on the same street. Her husband was a pastor and her baby was eight months old. She told me that Simon might not have problem with me associating with the lady since she is a good person and a pastor's wife. I was excited and agreed for the lady to visit me.

The first time the lady came to visit, Simon was at home. I introduced her to Simon. He left us alone in the living room. She stayed for about half an hour and left because the visit was not scheduled. She promised to schedule a time when we could meet and suggested we could then go to a mother and baby club at the end of our street.

As soon as she left, Simon started interrogating me. He asked, "Where is she from? Where does she live? Is she married? What does she do? What did you talk about? How many times has she been to the house?" I answered all the questions to the best of my knowledge. I told him that that was her first visit and it was the first time I've seen and spoken to her. I have never met her husband and never been to her house. I told him all I knew, which was all that my Health Visitor had told me about her. He did not believe me. Simon started yelling that he had warned me that he didn't want me to have friends. He reiterated that he didn't want her to visit me again. I tried persuading him that it's ok for me to have friends. She seemed like a very nice lady; plus I could think and reason for myself and nobody could deceive me. He refused to see my point.

It had been a few weeks since I'd seen the neighbour. She was passing by and decided to drop by to see me. As it happened again, Simon was at home. He let her in the house but remained in the living room with us. He walked aimlessly back and forth from the living room to the kitchen. She didn't even stay fifteen minutes before she left. I guess she sensed the tension and did not feel comfortable. As soon as she left, Simon started yelling that he had warned me to tell her not to visit me or speak to me again. He was so mad that I hadn't listened to him. I tried explaining and pleading with him that her visit was not planned. I went on to tell him that I had been looking for the right opportunity to tell her not to visit me and this was the only time I had seen her since her first visit and it would have been my opportunity to tell her because I didn't have her telephone number, but he would not listen. Instead, Simon started threatening me. He got a piece of A4 paper and a pen and began to write something. He wrote half way and then got another piece of paper and handed me the pen. He asked me to copy what he had written on the fresh piece of A4 paper. He had written a letter to the lady. He threatened me to copy it or be beaten. As I sat there, with him standing over me, copying what he had written, tears were falling down my face. I kept thinking the impact that letter would have on the lady and her husband. I kept thinking she would think I am a bad person. In the letter, which he forced me to copy, he wrote things in this context "Dear ...X, my husband is not happy with me having friends, especially with people from Ghana. Please stop visiting and calling me because you are causing my husband and I distress ...etc." When I finished copying what he had written, he asked me for her address which I supplied. He got an envelope, put the letter inside, sealed it, put a first class stamp on it and went to a post box a few yards from our house and sent it off.

Two days later my Health Visitor, who is also a Ghanaian came and I told her about the letter. I begged her to apologise to the lady on my behalf and explain that I could never write such a letter to her. I wanted her to know that Simon wrote it and forced me to copy it. My health visitor told me she already explained to the lady that it was definitely Simon who had written the letter. I learnt from my Health Visitor that the letter had caused serious problems between the lady and her husband. Her husband, in turn, banned her from walking past my house. She had to take a longer route to and from shops, the bus stop, doctor's office and everywhere that involved going past our house. So that was it. Simon had won again. That was the end of our friendship before it even began.

About two or three months after the letter incident, Simon came home one day and told me that he saw the lady who came to visit me a few months ago. She was at the bus stop and he helped her put her pushchair in the bus. I could not believe what I heard. I was upset and told him that if he thought playing the good guy would make the lady view me as the bad person then he was mistaken. The lady already knew it was him who wrote the letter, not me. I told him he was a hypocrite and that wiped the smile off his face. He had tried to make me feel bad, but it hadn't worked.

When my baby was eight months old, Simon agreed to enrol me into college part-time. By this time I had started going to church on Sundays, but not regularly. I got enrolled to study an Access to Law course in preparation for a Law degree, which Simon wanted me to study. I had a background in sciences, but if the only way I could go to college was to study what he wanted me to, I was willing to do that. It was for my sanity and to just have a touch of interaction with the outside world.

On the first day of college I was excited and eager and got ready on time. I also got the baby and his things ready. Simon had agreed to look after him for the rest of the day as planned. As I walked up to open the front door and head towards college, the next thing I heard was Simon's loud voice as he asked harshly, "Where do you think you are going?" I answered quietly, "To college" while turning slightly to face him. Still in a raised harsh voice he charged towards me asking, "Who is going to look after the baby...?" He also said something else that I could not figure out. That was because before he finished speaking he punched me so hard on my forehead that I passed out. When I came round, I found myself leaning against the front door and the wall beside it. My hands were on my head. The bag that had been on my right shoulder was now on the floor. I was dazed and in excruciating pain. I could not believe what he had done. In order to prevent further abuse that morning, at just 7am, I picked up my bag and staggered to the living room to have a seat. I was still holding my head with one hand and in so much pain. He walked into the living room after me. He was still cussing but since he saw that I was in no shape to speak or fit for further beating he left me there. I lay on the couch for a while before getting up to take some painkillers to help with my throbbing headache. The pain was getting increasingly worse as the shock wore off. That day was the end of the college I had been promised. It ended on the first day even before it started.

The emotional, verbal and mental abuse continued. He had now extended the insult to my whole family and would call them beggars. He began using the promises to wed and educate me as trophies that he had won by refusing to fulfil them. Every now and then he would use the promises as a way to make me obedient. He'll let me know that he may fulfil his promises if I remained implicitly obedient.

Whenever Simon felt like it he would cause an argument and use that as an excuse not to buy food for the house. He would claim that I shouldn't make him upset and that if I didn't, he would get food. On these occasions, if there was only rice in the house, that's all I would eat for breakfast, lunch and dinner. Sometimes this lasted for a week or more usually or until I got fed up and stopped eating all together. He'd buy just milk and tinned food for the baby and eat out.

I complained about his abuse to him. I just needed to be heard and hoped I could break through to him. All he would do is threaten me some more. On one occasion I was holding the baby and complaining about his behaviour when he stood up and reached to punch me in the face. I ducked at first and told him to mind the baby. Then he reached out again to punch me. As I tried to cover my face the baby fell and cut his eyebrow on the radiator in the living room. It just barely missed his left eye. I turned away from Simon and ignored him. As I was attending to my bleeding baby, he started blaming me for the baby's injury. That scar is still on my son's eyebrow to this day. It is a reminder of what happened and it saddens me.

Once again, we lived on.

*Violence is the last refuge
of the incompetent.*

– Salvor Hardin

CHAPTER LESSONS

Abuser's Controlling Tactics

1. Social isolation.
2. Blaming you for making him abuse you. Abusers make you feel like it was your fault.
3. False apologies.
4. No concern for children.

My Strategies

1. Confusion.
2. Hoping things will get better.

Could Have Done & Recommendations

1. Break isolation or leave.
2. Call Agencies that help women suffering domestic violence (details of such are in "Useful Contacts" section on "Surviving Domestic Violence Tips & Booklet". Download that booklet by visiting: www.survivingdomesticviolence.info or by emailing; felicity@felicityokolo.com

||||||||||||||||||||||||||||||||||||||||||||

CHAPTER FOUR

Spilling The Beans

At ten months old my son began to walk. He was enjoying life without a care in the world. He especially enjoyed getting my full attention. That was when Simon announced that it was time for me to have another baby. He instructed me to make an appointment with the doctor to remove my contraceptive coil so I could get pregnant. I told him it was too early for me to get pregnant and it would be best for the baby to be at least two years old before having another one. He insisted that now is a good time and it would be a good idea to have all our children close together. That way I would be free to go to college once the last one was five years old and in school. I was tempted to buy into the idea for one reason only. I loved the prospect of going to college and the freedom it might give me but we just couldn't agree on the number of children we wanted. This really put me off and made me doubt his plan. At this point, I still believed that things might get better. I wanted three children and he wanted five to seven kids. That scared me and I told him there was no deal.

Simon's response to my insistence that five to seven children were too many didn't go down well. As usual, he resorted to threatening me. He said I must take off my contraceptive coil and become pregnant the following month or else. I did not want to find out what 'or else' meant. To prevent further trouble I made appointment to have the coil removed.

Thankfully I did get pregnant again quickly. I found it hard to look after the first baby, myself and do my responsibilities for the house and tenants too. To make it more difficult I had to deal with Simon. He was always complaining. He called me names and said that I was lazy, useless, dirty, no good etc. Any bad thing he could think of came out of his mouth on a more regular basis. The abuse was getting worse but there was no physical violence. The abuse came in the forms of emotional, verbal, financial, and mental.

One day he returned from work and started complaining that I had not cleaned the house. The reason, he suspected, was because I watched too much TV. I tried to explain to him that I was struggling with the pregnancy and the baby. I needed help and a break sometimes, which I wanted him to give to me. Before I finished speaking he went into the kitchen and came back with a knife and cut off the TV cable. I was hurt and felt that my only means of keeping in touch with the outside world has been disconnected. I did not say a word.

The next day, while Simon was out, I wanted some entertainment so I decided to fix the TV. Thank God for O'Level Physics and all the knowledge gathered from watching my elder brother work with wires in my family home. I found an old cable with a plug somewhere in storage and connected the wires to that of the TV. I sealed it with sticky backed plastic.

When Simon returned he was surprised to see me watching the same TV he had disconnected. He asked me what I did. I told him to take a look for himself. When he saw what I did he laughed and almost applauded me. I reminded him that one of the reasons he married me was for my intelligence and I'd not lost it. I went on to tell him that if only he would let me be myself and take off all barriers I could do more and we could have more. He said no. He didn't like that. Simon expressed that he preferred me to stay at home and do what he tells me to do. I also reminded him that I was a University student; plus a TV and Radio actress before he married me. I added that I would like to go back to college, act and sing. He laughed even louder this time and told me he would never allow that. He went on to put down acting as work for loose men and women. He also told me that I would not be able to make it as a singer or actress in the UK. With that said, I began to tell myself that he might be right that I would not be able to make it as singer or actress in the UK. I told myself that I didn't know the procedures, I didn't have any formal acting or singing qualifications and I didn't have the accent. I believed him and shelved my dreams. As for college, I felt I still could make it, for nothing else but my sanity, if he lets me. I would not mind studying for a Law degree like he wanted me to.

All three bedrooms in the house had lodgers paying weekly rent. One couple, who paid monthly, paid by cheque directly to Simon. With all the money coming in from rent and his job I could not understand why he would not buy good nutritious food for us or why we were not well clothed. I did not know how much he earns from his job and I dared not ask. He complained about spending too much for the house already, but would not let me work to earn extra money.

Simon gave me £5 per week as my pocket money after much insisting about wanting some money of my own. He only gave me the pocket money during 'non-quarrelling' times. Whenever he made a complaint or found an excuse for an argument I would lose my pocket money that week. Since I wasn't allowed out, I began saving my pocket money until a leaflet came through the door with sample recipe cards. I used the money to pay for recipe cards of £4.95 once a month. Whatever money was left was used to buy things for trying out the recipes. It was the best way to have something different to eat and bake cookies for the children. Simon did not appreciate the new recipes. The children and I sure enjoyed them.

When the second baby was born, we could not agree on a name. We were still deliberating on names, or so I thought, when Simon came home one day with a birth certificate and two hideous names on it. I dare not mention them here. I was mad and couldn't believe what he did. He claimed that it was his right to call the children whatever he pleases. I reminded him that the children are humans with feelings and that any name is just not good enough; especially calling them some military word for a name. I did not know what to do, neither did I know where to register a birth because he registered the first baby with the names we agreed on. Previously, I had no cause to know the procedure but now I wanted to know. I did not like the name but got used to calling the child that name.

Now, with the second baby and the recent disrespect, I made up my mind not to have any more children with him. He couldn't afford to look after us and he sure didn't care or spend time with the children or me. I also had to try and protect all of us from the abuse. So I decided to break all the rules he made and do whatever I wanted when I wanted to. I believed that if I obeyed all the rules I deserved to be treated nicely, should be respected, and well provided for; certainly loved. Since none of those things were forth coming I decided to do the opposite. I would not be so obedient to this man who was full of lies and hatred. I told him all of this to his face. I also expressed that I didn't care if the marriage worked anymore because I had given my all and all he did was abuse me. I was through and I'd had enough. I told him that if he didn't start to buy food I would start to beg his friends and anyone possible.

I did not make threats. I made promises that I planned to keep. So when he refuses to buy food because I did not do what he wanted, I called his friends and distant relatives and told them. They would call and speak with him about the situation. I hoped they would scold him for not buying food for his family.

Before I married Simon I had learned how to manage my anger. I had taught myself to eliminate anger from my life when I was 18. Simon knew that whatever he did, I found it hard to get angry and this annoyed him a lot.

However, when Simon transferred the abuse that had been directed to me to the children – his lack of care for them and especially remembering when he locked me out when the first baby was soaked with urine to his clothes, that's when something inside of me changed. It was the natural motherly instincts within me. The ones designed to protect my offspring at all costs. It took charge and I was prepared to do anything to protect my children. This included becoming angry when it was necessary.

As I reflected on my life before Simon I realised that I couldn't even recognise myself. Before marrying him and coming to England, I was a university student and a part-time actress on national TV and Radio stations in Borno State. Now, this is what I had been reduced to. I was a prisoner and a slave in a foreign country. I was far, far away from home without friends and family. This life was nowhere near close to what I expected from a marriage and didn't fulfil anything I'd envisioned for myself. I kept praying he would have a change of heart. I kept thinking I could change him by loving him more and obeying all the rules. I kept praying he would stop taking out his fear and anger from his previous marriage unto me. I kept praying until I was numb. The answer did not come to me or maybe I did not hear it. I soon discovered that it wasn't necessarily his fear and anger from his previous marriage that made him behave the way he did. Simon was just acting the way he was.

I thought about Simon and what I'd been able to learn about him the past years. He had won the divorce case between him and his ex-wife. All he had to pay her was £4000 lump sum and that was nothing when you considered the value of a three-bed maisonette in East Dulwich. He still continued being abusive towards me. I found out he did not get on with his parents, brothers and sisters except the sister who introduced us. Basically he was a man living in a world of his own. The so-called "friends" of his were just two men; one with family and the other was single. They seldom visited or called him. There were some distant relatives whom he called on occasions, but they hardly called him.

The Revelation

During one argument I accused him of not caring for the children or me. I told him he must not have a heart or else he wouldn't let us starve. That's when he revealed the true reason why he married me. He told me he married me to have children so he could save his house. He went on to say that his barrister, whom he views like a god, had told him that to prevent his ex-wife from getting her rightful share in their divorce proceeding he must remarry and have children quickly. This was because the property was listed in both their names. The barrister was able to put together a strong case for Simon now that he was remarried with children. That fact allowed for the argument that it would be wrong for the court to want to sell the property and give half the equity to the ex-wife. It would certainly be unfair to ask Simon to pay his ex-wife any maintenance since he has a new family responsibility and had little income.

I didn't know whether to laugh or cry after hearing this revelation. I wanted to be angry and I wanted to keep my cool. It was so frustrating. I ignored my desire to attack him and just remained speechless. Once again, Simon had my head spinning. At least it wasn't from an actual punch this time.

After I recovered from the bombshell I told him that I could take him using me but not the children. I told him that it is disturbing to learn that he is having children just to save his house. That's it, I couldn't live with you anymore. You are using the children and I. You don't love or care for us and there is no need to stay with you, I said to him.

Simon's words were burning in my mind. All day long I kept thinking about what he had said. I kept thinking about what I could do and where I could go? I did not have any skills or qualifications so I decided to stay in the house until I come up with a plan.

I couldn't understand Simon's purpose in life. He was prepared to abuse and use three people just to get what he wanted. I wondered what else he might do and that was a very scary thought.

Even with this information, I wasn't that scared. My spirit was perturbed and my survival instincts kicked in. My courage level was starting to soar and I knew where I stood.

I stood on my own. As a mother of two beautiful children I was ready to make the changes that would ensure not only our survival, but also a better life. The life we all deserved, my children and I.

I kept praying and listening to music. They were such a good escape for me. I began attending church regularly, taking the children to the park and attending a baby and toddler group close to the house. I was actually interacting with people. Everything that he prevented me from doing before, I was now doing and it felt good. Whenever he refuses to buy food, I'll call one of his friends or wait till a tenant pays rent to me when he was not around. I would use that money to buy food and things the children needed.

I enrolled for a six weeks swimming course once a week and had one of the lodgers babysit for me. Simon still disapproved and didn't want to offer any help. I attended another six-week course in flower arranging. The next course was in facial care and another in touch-typing. A crèche was provided in all the courses except swimming. I did all these things just to interact with other people but swimming and touch-typing turned out to be two of the most valuable life skills for me.

Simon definitely started to take notice that I was determined to do what I wanted to do and I didn't care if he agreed or not. He slowly began to turn a blind eye to what I was doing and ignored me most of the time. Occasionally, he would drive me to church or show up at the park while the children and I were there. Then he would brag about this to his friends that he was the perfect husband and father.

While he said those words I could see through him and new his true motives. He wanted to make sure I was actually going to church and to the park like I said. That was better than going to another man's place or hanging around with friends that didn't make his approval list. The list was obviously very elite because there was not a single person on it – not even him.

I started taking driving lessons once per fortnight from a professional driving instructor. I paid for the lessons from the money I saved from my £5 per week pocket money. When Simon felt like it he would give me practice lessons between my lessons with the instructor. They usually ended up in arguments.

Now that I knew I was on my own I started to stand up to Simon during arguments. I was well prepared to defend the children and myself whenever he threatened violence; especially after one incident when he smacked our first child so badly that it went way beyond discipline. It was abuse and I promised to call the police if he repeated that.

With my newfound courage and 'freedom' I told Simon I would like to go back to college. As usual, he wanted me to study what he wanted and I agreed. I found a college that offered a part-time one-year course in "Access to Legal Studies" which would eventually lead to a law degree at a university. He agreed for me to attend and paid the initial fee of about £200. I was pleased to have the opportunity to challenge my brain before I became brain dead from abuse. I did not mind studying anything I could just so I could get out of the house. The course was for two days a week 6-9pm.

I was excited to go to college and I prayed he would keep his promise this time. All he needed to do was babysit the children while I attended classes. I had asked for nothing more. On my first day of college I was surprised he came home on time and I headed for college.

On my second day of college, I got the children ready and prepared to leave on time, but he did not come home. He did not have a mobile phone then and there was no way of contacting him. I waited. Simon finally came home at 6:30 p.m. He'd completely disregarded that he was supposed to be home at 5:30 p.m and take me to class for 6:00 p.m.

I sensed that he didn't want me to go to college. Since I knew I was on my own, my whole outlook had changed. I refused to let him stop me. A bulldozer couldn't have stopped me because I was very determined. So as soon as he walked in the house I picked up my college bag and headed off to class. I wouldn't dignify his actions with any questions about why he was late. Besides, I was already late enough.

On my return, I asked him why he hadn't come home on time but he could not give me any good reason. He didn't feel he owed me one either. The following week he came home late on both days I was supposed to attend my classes. That meant I was late again.

By the third week, I decided not to wait for him. My neighbours were at the rescue. My neighbours were a family of five: Tony, Sue, Lyn, Tracy and Alex. Tracy did not live with her parents and sisters, but visited often. If I didn't see Simon by 5.30pm, I went to my neighbours and begged them to babysit the children 'till he got home. If Sue and any or her daughters were home, Lyn or Alex would babysit while she drove me to college. If only one of them was around I would take the bus and end up really late.

Like I mentioned, my course ran from 6pm-9pm. Arriving at 7pm or later was really late, but I did not mind because I was determined to complete the course. To avoid disrupting the class, I explained my circumstance to my lecturer who understood and admired my determination.

A month into my course I discovered I was pregnant with my third baby. This was a very big surprise. I had promised myself not to have any more children with Simon. I also had my contraceptive coil.

When my doctor found out I was pregnant because the coil had moved she wanted to see Simon a.s.a.p. She was furious and immediately picked up the phone and called him at home to come to the surgery immediately. The surgery was about seven minutes walk from home. After 15 minutes of wait he had not showed up and when she called again, there was no answer. She then told me that she wanted Simon around to discuss termination of the pregnancy. She warned that since I was not well fed and looked after with two children under three years old, she feared that my body would not be able to cope with a third pregnancy. My health was also at risk.

I was in tears and surprised to hear about the pregnancy. The doctor went on to say that the pregnancy was about six weeks old and I did not have long to think about a termination. She asked me what I wanted to do but I could not answer. I later told her I didn't know and would discuss it with Simon. The doctor and other health personnel at the surgery already knew about my problems at home from my health visitor. I guessed that I was high risk on their books and that's why I wasn't surprised when the doctor reacted the way she did.

When I got home, I told Simon what the doctor suggested. He was strongly against it. I found it hard to make up my mind. Apart from my health risks, my main concern was bringing another child into a home where he or she was not wanted. Simon had not held back on telling me that. I also battled with my religious beliefs against terminating a pregnancy.

I cried and prayed for a decision but could not make up my mind. The thought about the impact of this pregnancy on my health and my education that I had just started would be severe. I had no doubt about it. I had been dying for outside activity to keep my sanity and the effect of another child on my current children worried me. Simon didn't give them enough attention. Still, I couldn't figure out what to do.

After three months of confusion and morning sickness finally over, I decided to keep the pregnancy. I truly believed that there was a higher reason why this baby had to live and I decided on a name for it. I asked God to make a way out for me from the abusive marriage I was in. I wanted to raise my children in a happy, loving home, but with Simon around that would not be possible.

The verbal and emotional abuse got even worse with my third pregnancy. I was struggling to look after the two other children, my health was poor and now I had college to deal with as well. Simon added a new insult by calling me a prostitute because I refused to have sex with him. He accused me of sleeping with one of our lodgers who helped babysit for me on occasions. The lodger would help me out when I needed a break from the two children every now and then or if I needed to get to the shops quickly. Simon kept claiming that the third pregnancy was not his but that of the lodger. How convenient I thought to myself. All this was making my life more unbearable.

When I was six months into the pregnancy, Simon started driving me to and from college. He had finally realised that I would stick by my commitment to college no matter what.

I was determined but I could not conquer the depression that I was feeling from the abuse and exhaustion. One night he punched me in the face again and I just walked out of the house. I started to contemplate suicide and was starting to believe that would be my only escape. I walked around the streets aimlessly and could not stop crying. I went to the church I attended but they would not hear me out. I think they believed me to be mad or drunk. Without knowing what else to do, or who to ask for help, I called the police from a payphone. They advised me to call "The Samaritans". The Samaritans were an organisation that helped people contemplating suicide. (Their details are in the useful contacts sections in the ebook "Surviving Domestic Violence Info & Tips" which you can get from www.survivingdomestic-violence.info) They had a free phone number for me to call that was displayed on the payphone box. The Samaritans calmed me down and counselled me against suicide. They reminded me of the many reasons to live based on what I told them about my life. They also gave me a number to call for emergency shelter because I did not want to return home that night.

I spent that night in the shelter and it gave me a bit of time alone to think. The next day I called Simon and asked him to pick me up somewhere close to the shelter. I returned home. Now I had a request in to God to help get me out of the house within a year. I asked for a year because I knew the baby would have arrived by then and I would have recovered from the delivery. Then I would leave and go anywhere else besides back there.

* * *

I completed my course two weeks before my third baby was born. He was a gorgeous big baby who spent five days in intensive care because of his weight. During the first three days of his life, he was fed by tube because he could not suck on anything and he also had his heel pricked every 2-3 hours to monitor his blood sugar level. This was a big concern for me and it made me anxious. He was released from intensive care on the fifth day and kept for observation in the ward with me.

That same day, my Auntie was visiting me. She asked me if we had a name for the baby. I told her that we had not yet decided and based on the original agreement I made with Simon, I would get to call the baby an English name and Simon would get to give the baby an Ibo name. Just then

Simon walked in and I told him that my Auntie asked about the baby's name. I told him how I was just telling my Auntie about the agreement we had made. Before I could finish speaking Simon excitedly smiled and said to me, "Oh you don't have to worry about a name. I have already registered the baby." I was shocked and would have been instantly angered if I had the energy. I asked him when and he replied, a few days ago. Then I asked him what the name was and he mentioned some hideous name that would make a child contemplate suicide. This made me so mad that I exploded without knowing where the energy came from. I yelled, "What?" Then I reached out to a strong thick tumbler by my bedside unit. It was half filled with water and I was about to hit Simon with the tumbler when my Auntie restrained me. Simon ran out of the ward for fear of being hurt until my Auntie calmed me down. When he returned to the ward I told Simon I could not believe that while the baby was in intensive care all he did was register the baby with some hideous name. Especially since he didn't care if the baby lived or died. Also, what kind of a parent called their child a name that would make other children and adults tease them from birth 'till death. Anyone who hears the name is shocked to hear that a sane person would want to call his or her child such a name. The nurses who heard the commotion asked what the problem was and after I told them, they informed me that I could add another name to the birth certificate if I wanted. They also gave me the address of the registry office. I had never known that address until then.

After seven days in the hospital I finally returned home with my third baby. Simon and I continued where we left off.

I kept sinking lower the more the abuse elevated. I was so overwhelmed and my body was falling apart. I could barely do anything. I thought to myself that this was exactly what my doctor had been worried about. I remembered passing out once. It was during the birth of the third baby and I felt like I was going to die. I told my friend and neighbour Lyn who was with me, to make sure she told my other two children that I loved them so much and to say goodbye to them for me. I was so depressed that I wouldn't have minded dying during childbirth.

* * *

Two weeks after giving birth I had to take my driving test for the second time. It had been scheduled the previous month. I was pleased to have passed the test this time because it meant I could get about with all three children on my own.

That driver's licence was a step to freedom but it wasn't a step for lifting my depression. I just wanted to escape how I was feeling so I went to my doctor and complained I wasn't sleeping properly. My doctor gave me advice to help with the problem but refused to give me what I wanted - tranquilizers. She told me they would affect the baby because I was breastfeeding. I decided to buy the tranquillizers myself but the pharmacist would not sell them to me. I was told I had to get them on prescription. This was not good news and I cried all the way home because my intention was to take an overdose of the drug and die. I wanted a painless getaway from the world and my troubles but the world didn't want to let me go. There was some reason it wanted me to suffer and stick around. I didn't know what that reason was but I was so bitter about it.

I was forced to accept the fact that ending my life painlessly was not going to happen. I prayed to God to let me know the higher reason and pleaded for a quick reply. I also reminded myself that suicidal tendencies were higher in people under 25 years old. I would be over that threshold soon since I was already 24. I couldn't wait to be 25.

I did not bother sharing these suicidal tendencies with my family because they would not understand anyway. My neighbours – who are now my friends – and my Auntie were the only people who cared for my children and I. They were now my family. I found it hard to tell them about these feelings too.

In other to avoid any further surprise pregnancy, I enquired about a contraceptive that will give me 100% protection because I was desperate. A new contraceptive called Norplant was just out at that time. It guaranteed nearly 100% protection; it was just what I was looking for and it was what I settled for. It had a very serious side effect on me. I would bleed for almost two weeks every month. I did not mind as long as I did not bring any more unloved and uncared for children in the world with Simon. I was prepared to take my chances on Norplant's effectiveness. Also, it was supposed to last for five years.

Just three months after the birth of the third baby another big fight happened. It was bigger than any fight thus far. Simon beat me so badly with a stick that I had tried to use to defend myself that I could not move. At this time we had no lodgers and we occupied all the bedrooms upstairs. The dining room downstairs was being used for its intended purpose. I had insisted on that. Since the birth of the third child I was more scared than ever because I was not obeying any of his rules. I knew it was only a matter of time before Simon would be fed up with it. I decided to start keeping the back door unlocked. That way, if something happened, I would have a quick escape outside. Simon was not aware of that and I made sure that before going to bed I would check that it was unlocked every night. On the morning that Simon attacked me with the stick, he kept hitting me until I fell into the baby's cot. While I was lying in the baby's cot injured and helpless Simon kept hitting me. I called for my first child, who was only three years old, to go and call my neighbours. The children – the first and second, three and two years old respectively – witnessed me screaming while their father continued hitting me. This confused them and they began to cry.

My three year old, still crying, went downstairs and couldn't reach the front door. He came back up. I had to beg him to run and use the back door to get help very quickly. He did what I told him and as soon as my neighbours saw him in their back garden with pyjamas that morning they knew something was wrong. They didn't have to ask him what was wrong because they could hear me screaming.

Three of them; Tony, Sue and Lyn, quickly rushed upstairs to see Simon still hitting me with the stick. Tony pulled Simon away and almost hit him but his wife Sue

stopped him. They carried me out of the cot and laid me on
the bed and passed the phone onto me. I could not hold the
phone let alone dial 999; they had to hold the phone against
my mouth while I struggled to dial 999. The ambulance and
police came as quickly as they could and I was taken to hos-
pital while Simon was arrested.

My neighbours looked after the children while I was in
hospital. I gave a statement to the police while in there and
told them I wanted to press charges. My neighbours helped
me get a lawyer and a court date was set. I stayed with my
neighbours until the court hearing to avoid further attacks
from Simon and to recover. Lyn or Alex would sneak into
the house or escort me to my house when Simon was out to
pick up fresh clothing.

The date of the hearing was about two weeks after the
date of the incident. The judge asked me what I wanted and
I could not speak. The judge told me that if I wanted, he
could ask Simon to leave the house and put an injunction
against him coming close to me for my safety. He wanted to
know if that was okay with me. I still didn't know what to
do. He then said he could put an injunction against him be-
ing violent towards me and demand that he leave the master
bedroom, which we both shared and stay in a third bedroom.

I decided to settle for the lighter punishment for Simon
and did not press charges. Later I found out that so many
women do this and it is so unfortunate because it doesn't
stop the violence and abuse. Just like all the women before
me, my choice to be kind to Simon was a mistake that I lived
to regret. All I wanted was for Simon to stop hitting me and

I believed that not pressing charges and settling for a lighter punishment would deter him. I was wrong just like many other women.

After that court hearing I returned home from my neighbours' house and was feeling safe. I believed the court ruling would protect me. Simon moved to the spare bedroom in the house while the new baby and I stayed in the master bedroom. Simon was very bitter about this arrangement and very bitter about me taking him to court. He fumed around day and night and poured insults on me without hitting me. Simon knew the court ruling had a power of arrest attached and he knew that I did not have much say about it. He only had to threaten me and the police could come. He would be arrested because he would have broken court orders, not mine. He felt powerless for the duration of the order. It was for only six weeks.

During this period and in the weeks before the court hearing Simon and I were advised to attend mediation. I was up for it but he blatantly refused to attend. He said he would never attend such things and claimed that he did nothing wrong and didn't need help. He actually accused me of being the one who needed help on how to learn to implicitly obey him.

Simon now hated my neighbours so much for rescuing me and for helping me get lawyers that he even blamed them for breaking up his family. He could not wait for six weeks to be over and I kept kicking myself for not getting him out of the house and pressing charges. If only I had known that he would not appreciate what I did for him. Besides I was afraid he might come back into the house and kill the children and I because of the attachment he had with the property.

The six weeks went entirely too fast. As soon as the court injunction order expired, he started making further threats. I knew that with the current rage from the six weeks court injunction he could do worse to me. He was so bitter because he had to sleep in the spare bedroom that he decided to take off the lock from the master bedroom door where the youngest baby and I slept. I had locked the room every night since the injunction and now without the locks I did not feel safe. When Simon started threatening that what happened in the property will happen again; I knew there had to be more, maybe some dark secret the house held, apart from the abuse. After the threat kept repeating itself I finally decided to press my neighbours for a little history about our property. It turned out that the previous owner of the property shot and killed his wife and two children. Then he called the police and shot himself. He did not die but claimed insanity and was put in mental hospital. When I told Simon the story about the property from the neighbours, he confirmed it. He also added that he was ready to claim insanity should that happen to him so he would avoid going to prison. Simon was basically threatening to kill my children and I. He seemed to get some kind of sick thrill from what had previously happened at the property. I have never felt more unsafe.

Five months after the birth of my third child, Simon and I barely communicated with each other. Each of us did whatever we wanted to do. Knowing how dangerous the situation was, combined with Simon's threats; I was always on my guard to escape. I still had not figured out the best way to leave after I lost the opportunity during the court hearing.

The Escape

Simon was running late one evening. I had already cooked and eaten with the children. They were settled in bed and asleep. I was tidying up and getting ready to go to bed myself when Simon approached me. He wanted to cook his food, but the pots were dirty. He asked me to clean a pot for him. I told him he could clean any pot he wanted to use. He said he wanted to use the pot I had my food in. I told him that either way he would still have to clean the pot before using it so why not clean a different pot. He insisted on pouring out my food. I followed behind him and as he reached to the pot to pour out my food I grabbed the pot from him. I left the house and put the pot in the boot of my car. When I got back into the house Simon started threatening me. He said I must bring the pot back from my neighbours or else. He just assumed the pot was at my neighbours and since the last incident two months earlier, he could not bear to look at them. He even threatened them once.

I kept tidying up the kitchen and remained silent. Simon kept yelling repeatedly but I ignored him and refused to get angry back. I was doing the laundry as I cleaned everything up. The knob switch on the machine was broken. I had to use the pronged end of a hammer to pull out the knob to turn on the washing machine. I left the hammer on the washing machine to use for next wash. After the wash I put in was done, I put in the last wash before going to bed. After loading the last wash I could not find the hammer. I thought I misplaced it and went to get a knife or screwdriver instead. I just wanted to get to bed. I was so exhausted by that point and wanted the day to be done.

All the knives in the kitchen were gone, so were all the screwdrivers in the store. I asked Simon where they were. He ignored me and left the house. I left the wash in the washing machine and decided to go to bed. I had a bad feeling that Simon was thinking about attacking me with either a knife or screwdriver; perhaps something else even. I decided to sleep with my clothes on and my keys in my pocket so I could escape quickly if I needed to. With the lock off my bedroom door Simon could walk in anytime and corner me. This was especially possible if I was sleeping soundly.

At exactly 2:15 a.m. that night I felt my duvet get ripped off me. I woke up to see Simon standing over me. I remember looking at the clock immediately and that's how I knew the exact time. I was still drowsy when Simon started demanding, "Go and get that pot back or else." I forced myself to sit up in bed. By now his voice was raised and I could see the anger in his eyes. I told him that he would wake up the baby if he continued to talk so loudly. He didn't care. He continued to ask me to go and get the pot back. All the while he was blocking my way. I was now standing and thinking of the fastest way to get out. The room was on the first floor and the window faced the concrete garden in the back. I was afraid I would be hurt if I jumped. Just then the baby woke up. I blamed Simon for waking the baby. As he went over to the baby's cot I ran out of the room and climbed onto the front landing window. I was afraid to jump. Although there was grass on the ground nearby, I feared I might miss and end up on the concrete part of the front garden. He left the baby and starting throwing cold water at me to scare me into jumping so I would hurt myself. He didn't care and kept on with the taunting and cussing. The baby was crying again because he needed feeding. I told him that since he woke the baby up, he must pick him up and feed him. As soon as he went to pick up the baby, I got off the window and ran back into the house. I scrambled downstairs, grabbed my coat and ran out of the front door. I had just flip-flops on my feet. I jumped into my car and drove off so fast without my lights on because I didn't want him to be able to find and track me down. He dropped the baby and chased me with his own car. I drove three streets away from ours without lights and parked in-between cars and watched him drive slowly pass the street I was parked on. I slept in the car for the rest of that November night till 7am.

I woke my neighbours up at 7.30 a.m. that morning and told them what had happened. I added that I would never go back to live with Simon again. There was probably no need for me to tell them about the incident because they heard the noise and saw him chase me. I showered and ate breakfast there before they took me to a homeless shelter where I was given a temporal accommodation.

I stayed at the shelter for two days. It was extremely hard for me. I cried throughout my stay there and missed my children; especially the third baby who was still breastfeeding. I wanted my children and knew Simon couldn't look after them. Besides, he never wanted them in the first place and he was still planning to have a DNA test to confirm he was the father of the third baby. With same clothes on for two days in a row, I went back to my neighbours and told them I wanted to take the children. They advised me to get the police to escort me back to the house, which I did. I picked up the children, our clothes and the old TV set without remote control that I mended which was all that Simon allowed me to take. We left two new Nicam digital Televsions, the house and Simon for good.

We moved on.

Every trial endured and weathered in the right spirit makes a soul nobler and stronger than it was before.

– James Buckham

CHAPTER LESSONS

Abuser's Controlling Tactics

1. Forced pregnancy.

2. Breaking promises.

3. Isolation.

4. Verbal, emotional, financial and mental abuse.

5. Dream stealing.

6. Destroying your self-esteem

7. Destroy your self-confidence and belief in yourself.

8. Using the tool you used to protect yourself to hurt you

My Strategies

1. Obeyed rules hoping it would prevent further abuse.

2. Refused to have more children with abuser.

3. Made own rules.

4. Made mental preparation to leave.

5. Broke isolation.

6. Did whatever it took to look after myself.

7. Took driving lessons.

8. Attended free skills course/training that may come handy someday.

9. Threatened to report abuse on children if repeated.

10. Took a break from abuser.

11. Had an escape route ready for emergency escape.

12. Called the police and reported abuse.

13. Got medical help.

14. Used distraction to escape.

15. Left abuser.

16. Once out, used police escort to visit the house to prevent confrontation from the abuser and never believed to be safe with abuser without police escort.

Could Have Done & Recommendations

1. Avoid pregnancy.

2. Find out how the country system works to know about registering birth. Contact Citizens Advice Bureau to help with any issues or questions you may have about anything. If they are not able to help you directly, they will definitely direct you to the right agency to help you. This is a FREE service.

3. Get professional help to avoid contemplating suicide.

4. Take long breaks away from abuser by going to friends or family members.

5. Get some rest.

6. Get abuser to leave the house with an injunction and power of arrest.

PART TWO

Nothing is predestined:
The obstacles of your past can
become the gateways that lead
to new beginnings.

– Ralph Blum

CHAPTER FIVE

Christmas In Sheltered Housing

The confusion and unhappiness that plagued my life during my marriage to Simon, especially during my third pregnancy were quite intense I had hinted to my parents, my Auntie and Simon's cousin that I would leave Simon if he continued to abuse me. They all kept telling me it was teething problems that would soon go away and that such problems were typical of most marriages at the early stages. They also had the fear that it wasn't appropriate for people to go about airing their dirty linens in public.

I was now in a family shelter with my children. I had left Simon and called my Auntie and Simon's cousins to tell them. They were all shocked because of the age of the children. My Auntie said to me that if I was certain that's what I wanted and what would make me happy, then she would be there to support me as much as she could. I was happy to hear that she was willing to accept my decision and support me. I went on to tell her that the police and Housing Authority had told me not to tell anyone where I was staying at the moment because Simon was threatening to kill me and she understood. Simon's cousins on the other hand were very upset about my decision and asked me to go back to Simon. They said that women from Ibo land do not leave their husbands because of little fights and that there were many women who experienced worse than me, but did not leave. I told them that I have made my decision and it would stand because of my safety.

After I told my parents about leaving Simon they re-acted just like Simon's cousins. They yelled over the phone and threatened that if I didn't go back to Simon I should consider them no longer my parents. I explained to them that my mind was made up for my safety and besides I have given the marriage my best shot. I explained that despite my committed effort, my life was threatened several times and still under threat as we spoke. I went on to tell them that they did not know what it was like to be married to Simon because they were so far away. I concluded by telling them that if they wanted the marriage to continue then they could marry Simon instead. As for the threat of me considering them no longer my parents, it worked the first time when Simon came to marry me but it would NOT work this time or ever again. I told them I'd rather have no parents and be alive, than to have parents and be dead. With that said I put the phone down.

Communication between my parents and me did not take place for the next three years with only one exception when they called me about six months after I left Simon asking me to go back to him. I hung up on them just to avoid argument.

I felt alone, abandoned, rejected, unloved and punished for wanting to be alive and happy. I missed my parents, especially my mum but was angry with them at the same time. I also blamed them for everything that happened. They were the ones who made me marry Simon.

Simon was very upset to have lost control over me. When I went to pick up the children he specifically told me that I would not last two months in the UK without him and that I certainly would never be successful without him. He threatened that wherever I am he would find me and deal with me for breaking up his family. Simon also wanted me deported because my six months visa to join him was long expired. The Home Office had served both of us deportation orders after he applied for Indefinite Leave to remain in the UK. That order was refused. He felt that because he had lived in the UK longer than me and knew about the system, he would get our lawyer to appeal against the Home Office decision for himself only and that would leave me to be deported, since I was no longer with him.

I was in sheltered accommodations with my children for three months and could not tell my Auntie where I was or anyone else except my Health Visitor and old neighbours – Tony, Sue and Lyn. They brought us beddings, cooking pots and other things we needed that we didn't have. My Health Visitor had to make sure that the baby and other two children were well.

When my Health Visitor came for her first visit to the shelter, she opened my eyes to basic things that I had not considered necessary for our survival while living on my own with the children. She asked me how much money I was getting on Benefits from the Government and how I was spending it. At that time I was getting £81 per week spending money while the Council paid my rent and Council Tax. She asked me to start saving £10 per week from my spending money. I was apprehensive and told her that the money could barely buy food, nappies and petrol for the car; let alone leave extra to save. She pointed out that I must save for emergencies and also to buy necessary things I would need for my permanent accommodation: such as a refrigerator, washing machine, cooker and any other item necessary to start a household.

In the temporary accommodation we had two rooms with beds and wardrobes. There was a kitchen with a refrigerator, dining table and a cooker; plus a bathroom. My Health Visitor pointed out that the temporary accommodation had the basic furnishings but when we move to a permanent one, I would have to furnish it and buy those things myself. I was kind of disturbed that I would be faced with such expenses. I guess that was because I had moved straight from my parent's house to Simon's house. All of those things had always been in place for me. I had never had a chance to live on my own to discover that I would have to buy those things. I thanked her and started saving £10 per week. It was very difficult.

A week after I moved into my temporary accommodations also called a hostel, I was asked to apply for permanent accommodations and Benefits - government funds - to support my children and I since I had no income. I completed my application form and was invited for an interview. At the interview the baby was on my lap and the other children were flanked on each side. We sat there together and waited for our fate to be decided. In the application form I had intentionally omitted completing the section about immigration status because I was not sure what to write there. The interview entailed submitting my immigration documents to show I was a legal resident in the country. When the interviewer requested to see my documents I could not speak for fear of what would happen to us. When I summoned the courage to speak I told him the truth about my immigration status. I answered that I was waiting to hear from my lawyer about my case with the Home Office. He asked for evidence of what I just told him, such as any letter from my lawyer or Home Office but I could not supply any. He later explained to me that he could not process my application because I needed to have the right immigration documents or be born in the UK to be entitled for government Benefits. I just sat there thinking of how to survive with the children. I was almost in tears and focused on not breaking down. I didn't want to frighten the children. After staring at the children and I for a while, he asked me to leave because there wasn't much he could do without the right documents.

Somehow, just a week later, I received a letter approving my application for Benefits and Housing Benefits. I was also notified that I had been placed on waiting list for permanent accommodation. I was very pleased to receive the good news. The Benefits were very important because I was receiving emergency Benefits at that time and they were scheduled to stop in just two weeks.

I believe in divine intervention. I say that because I chose to be alive, rather than be killed because of fear of deportation. I believed that God would look after me and He surely did.

I remembered hearing about how a seven-month-old foetus in the womb could survive without the mother. I knew that anyone could survive without another person if that little person could. So whenever Simon started ranting about how I could not survive in the UK without him, I remembered that story and it kept me going. One day while still with Simon, I finally told him that story. I told him that I could survive without him; the children could survive without either of us and that as long as someone has the ability to breathe independently on their own, they could survive without anyone's help. I wasn't sure he understood but I was happy that my beliefs and theories were paying off now.

The hostel I was in was filled with women with children. Most of them had similar experiences like mine, some even worse. On my second or third day there, an Italian lady asked me what I was in there for. I forced a chuckle and said to her that she made it sound like a prison? She said it might as well be since we were all hiding for our safety. I told her a summary of my story and she told me hers. She asked me how long I was married for and I told her. She went on to tell me that she had been married for 20 years to her abuser. I was stunned to hear that she had endured domestic violence for 20 years. I thought four and half years was bad, but for 20 years? I asked her why she decided to leave now. She said she wasn't sure. She had just felt that she was advancing in age and that her body could no longer take the beating. Besides that, her children were beginning to disrespect her for tolerating the abuse and for allowing them to live through it in their young lives. Her children were 12-19 years old, two boys and two girls. I could not believe that someone could live in an abusive relationship for 20 years. I knew four and half years with Simon was too much; let alone 20 years.

I stayed as long as I did because I was too weak most of the time to make a move. Every year I was either pregnant or nursing a baby while with Simon. I had also been afraid to leave because of my lack of means for income, plus my immigration status. As soon as I realised that Simon was using all those things to his advantage to continue abusing me; I refused to tolerate it. I left based on my theory about the seven month old unborn baby and my belief that God makes way where there seems to be no way. I was comforted to remember an Ibo proverb my mum used to say. It said, "God chases flies for a cow without a tail". I've always heard that proverb but it never made much sense to me 'till now. Now I was a woman who was living that proverb.

The Italian lady was the only woman I was close to in the hostel. She was about 44 while I was 24. I felt like she wanted to mentor me by telling me how to treat John, a man I just met as described in chapter six. I refused to let her mentor me because I didn't want a mentor whose actions did not reflect what they preached. While she was kind, what she preached was not in alignment with what I wanted in my life.

My Italian friend was very nice to my family. Both she and her children helped babysit for me when I went out which was about once a week or once every fortnight. She had also started dating a man whom she claimed was her childhood sweetheart. He was slapping her around and married to someone else too. I couldn't understand why she allowed that and I just found it hard to respect her. She had experienced 20 years of abuse and was now in a shelter and getting some more. When I asked her why she tolerated violence from her so called childhood sweetheart, she did not have a good answer. She shrugged it off and said that he loves her and that he was a very nice man who was frustrated with his wife. She went on to say that he was just waiting for a good excuse to leave his wife and come to her. I was disappointed but did not convey it to her. I felt she had had enough troubles and frustrations in her life already and I didn't need to add to the burden.

Even though I was at the starting point of a fresh new start, I was still very depressed and tired. I had been in my temporary accommodations for about two weeks and was so sick of living on barely anything. It wasn't like I had much less than I had before. I just didn't realise the costs of living on my own and being responsible for three children. Plus, I didn't have any healthy relationships to develop with the ladies around me. Most of them were in the same situation as me – they were trying to figure out their new lives free of domestic violence. I had fewer breaks from the children than ever before. I was still breastfeeding the baby and that exhausted me even more. I became frustrated and felt that at 24 years old I was too young to be burdened with so much responsibility and to feel so much pain. I decided that I needed a quick way out. I thought hard about what to do and realised I was now free to live as I wanted without Simon to control me and I didn't need my parents approval any longer. I felt some sort of happiness to learn about my newfound freedom. I thought to myself that if I was not able to get help to end my life the last time, what made me think I'd get help now. I kept reminding myself that I'd be 25 soon and once I hit that age, all suicidal tendencies would go away. I was still confused and I believed I needed sometime to myself to get clarity on what to do.

So I called Sue and told her that I had decided to give the children up to the Council to look after for a while. I explained that I needed to sort myself out – whatever that means. She was not happy with me giving up the children; she explained to me that there were other ways. She went on to tell me that whoever would look after the children will not do as good of a job than me their mum. She also said that the children may end up being damaged and may not have good relationship with me later in life if I gave them up at such a young age; an age when they needed me the most. I thought she had a point, but I argued that I was overwhelmed and beginning to lose my temper with the children and I didn't feel that I was good for them either. She informed me that she had an idea and asked me to meet her at the local Council Office the next day.

We met that day at the Council Office as planned. I was so nervous and confused, so unsure of what was going to happen and what I wanted to do that I found it hard to park the car and ended up scratching the side of it in my panic.

Once in the Council Office, Sue and I met with a Council Officer. This person explained what options I had available. Sue asked for immediate help for me as soon as possible. I was given a kind of help that they called 'respite care' at the time. This entailed me taking the two older children to a child minder from 8 a.m. – 6 p.m Monday thru Friday for three weeks so I could have time to rest. I thought to myself, what about the baby? Since the baby was less than six months old the service did not include him. Sue persuaded me to take this offer and I did. I was also referred to counsellors in my area and I started having counselling to deal with my emotions and pains.

The following week I started taking the two older children to a child minder of my choice. When I returned to the hostel with the baby I just went to sleep. I had to stop breastfeeding earlier than I wanted because I was not well fed and I was getting very lethargic.

Two weeks into the 'respite care' I gained so much energy and had time to think. Although plagued with all unsupportive circumstances and an overwhelming feeling that all odds were against me, I was somehow able to reach down and find my dreams again. The dreams I had of being a show biz star surfaced. I remembered a lady telling me I was heading for Hollywood whenever she saw me on TV and on campus carrying a guitar. Dreams of being a microbiologist and the dreams of having a happy, loving successful life were all coming back to me. They were being resurrected now. I wanted to live again. I decided life was well worth living no matter my current situation. I knew the circumstances would not last forever. Just like the marriage only lasted four and half years. Yes, that time seemed like an eternity of hell but I was out, alive and free to live again. It was what I had always dreamed about.

I was amazed at how a little break made all the difference for my outlook on my life and the choices I could make. All I needed was some time to myself to think and get some rest before my dreams all flowed back to me. I realised what a mistake it would have been if I had given my children away. I felt blessed to have Sue there to offer an alternative.

I wasn't sure how to pursue my show biz career. So I decided the first thing to do was to go back to university and obtain a degree that would enable me get a good job that paid well so I would be able to look after the children and myself.

So there I was, a month after leaving Simon, depressed and under threat of deportation and my life under threat by Simon. I was surviving on £81 per week and not sure if I could furnish my flat when I moved in or how I would celebrate Christmas with my children. Still, I had a sense of freedom and joy. I called four universities for their prospectuses just before Christmas. I did not have a clue when applications should be submitted or when admission was done but I knew what I wanted and I just did it. Luckily, there was a publication of a University League Table that was just released. I found that it came as an attachment with a newspaper I picked up in our temporary accommodations shared laundry room. I used the League Table to decide the four best universities to apply for that ranked first to fourth. At that time they were Oxford, Cambridge, Imperial College and Kings College respectively. I was so excited that I was free to do what I wanted and it felt good.

I began to love myself again, to appreciate my life and feel the joy of my dreams already accomplished even though I had just resurrected them.

For Christmas that year, my Health Visitor brought presents for the children from Barnados charity all wrapped up. It was just three days until Christmas. This helped a lot and meant that I did not have to worry about buying any presents. For me the joy of calling for university prospectuses combined with the sense of freedom were enough presents. I took the children to church on Christmas day and prepared rice afterwards. We ate that rice with love and in peace, just the four of us. That was probably the best Christmas I ever had since I came to England. It was simply because we shared love and had peace.

We survived on.

You can't cross the sea merely by standing and staring at the water.

– Rabindranath Tagore

CHAPTER LESSONS

Abuser's Controlling Tactics

1. Threatened to kill me.

My Strategies

1. Blamed others.
2. Thought of giving the children away as an escape.
3. Saved money - at least 10% of 'income or benefits'.
4. Kept temporary address secret.
5. Had strong faith & belief in God.
6. Got 'respite care'.
7. Resurrected dreams.
8. Rested.
9. Applied to universities to kick start independence.
10. Began to love myself again to increase my self-esteem.
11. Began to appreciate my life again

Could Have Done & Recommendations

1. Not blame others but take responsibility.
2. Take self-defence classes.
3. Asked for help from agencies or government before thinking of giving the children away.

CHAPTER SIX

Dating Again?

The time for my 'respite care' to end was fast approaching. One evening as I was walking back home with my children after picking them up from the child minder, when a man walked up to me and introduced himself. He wanted to walk us home but I did not let him because I did not know him. I instantly became suspicious he perhaps knew Simon. Simon had been wondering where I was and I feared this man was sent to find out where we were staying.

The next day he came up to me after I dropped off the children in the morning. He said he was interested in me and calmed my fears about Simon and where I was staying. Once again, he showed up the next day. He came up to me and this time I let him walk with me to my temporary accommodation. I gave him an audience there and wanted to know why he was interested in me.

Dating was the last thing on my mind at this time, besides I somehow believed what Simon had told me that no man would want me with three children, that they'll just want me for sex and no one would want to look after another man's children.

I knew I didn't want to depend on someone to look after my children or me and that's why I had applied to obtain a degree. I had also decided to raise my children on my own to ensure a happy, loving home and I did not think that having a man around who was not their father would help at that time. They were so young and they didn't deserve to be involved in the conflicts that were inevitable in a relationship. I made a firm decision to raise them to school age before looking at any serious relationship.

I informed John about my decision and why. I also told him about my experience with Simon. He said he understood but he still wanted to date me. He went on to say that he admired my courage and determination to leave Simon and raise the children on my own. He complimented me on wanting to go back to university. He went on to tell me that those were the reasons why he wanted to be around me and that I was also an admirable woman.

I could not help but like the attention and decided to go out on a date with him. We went to the movies and that was my first time going to a cinema. It felt weird and I felt so strange going out somewhere without the children. I had not gone out alone with Simon the entire time we had been together.

When I was out on my date, I sort of felt like I had lost the children. It was a weird sensation, but I liked it and wanted more of it. We went out the following week again and I shared my dreams with him. I also expressed my fears about forming a new relationship after being involved in an unhappy violent one so recently. I notified him that if any misunderstanding should arise between us, he must not raise his voice in front of the children or where they could hear him. My beautiful children had witnessed enough violence to last them a lifetime. I was prepared to do whatever it took to prevent exposing all of us to violence again. He agreed to these conditions. I had said I wouldn't go on another date until he did. He agreed to all my conditions and encouraged me to keep pursuing my dreams.

I did not want the children to know about John yet, so he visited me while they were away to the child minder. Sometimes he came at night while they were in bed. When we did go out, Lyn would come and babysit or the lady I'd grown close with in temporary accommodations would. It was very nice to have friendships with women and with my new freedom I was beginning to feel like I had a great chance at happiness.

* * *

Just after Christmas I finally received the university prospectuses and soon found out I had to study for a year to obtain an Access qualification. It was only then that I could proceed to university. This was because I did not have any Advanced (A) Level qualifications. I also found out that my first and second University choice, which were Oxford and Cambridge, were not in London. If I wanted to attend any of them I would have to move out of London. I did not want to do that. I was left with my third and fourth choices. They were Imperial College and Kings College respectively. I chose Imperial College as my preferred college and worked towards securing admission there.

I continued dating John, taking the two older children to the child minder, saving £10 per week, getting counselling and trying to get a grasp on everything that was going on. It all seemed like a dream. Suddenly, I had three children to care for alone. I was depressed to the point of giving away my children. My parents and family had abandoned me. I was in a hostel hiding for my safety. While all those things were happening I was applying to go to the university in hopes of a better future. Plus, I was dating a man again.

I had so many things going on and I wanted them all. Still, nothing made sense. I was not sleeping properly again because of all the emotions and stress. When John was around, he would run me a hot bath at night. He was so kind trying to help me sleep better. He was not allowed to spend the night at my place. That was one of my rules. As confused as I was, I did not want the children to be also confused seeing him staying the night. They were too young and so was our relationship.

John, at that time, was just completing his Ph.D. research in a city in the outskirts of London. That meant he had to be away every now and then. It was nice to have him around but I still had my suspicions as to why he wanted to be around me. We talked mostly about me and very little about him. He was not willing to talk about himself and kept saying it was more important to focus on me. He was probably in his late thirties at that time. I was just guessing. When I had asked him his age he told me he was as old as Simon. When I asked him if he was married, he said no. When I asked if he had children he said no. I was not satisfied with his answers about himself because I felt a man of his age who was also from Africa was expected to be married with children by his age. Although I was not satisfied with his answers, even after asking him about a wife and children, I let it go and focused on my problems at hand. I already knew that I was not ready for a long-term relationship at that time. Still, I did not want to date a married man either. There was no way of me knowing otherwise because he lived with his sister while in London. His sister was the only member of his family that I knew and we did not get to speak on a personal level.

And so I lived on.

Strength does not come from physical capacity. It comes from an indomitable will.

– Mohandas Gandhi (Mahatma Gandhi)

CHAPTER LESSONS

Abuser's Controlling Tactics

1. Threat to kill.

2. Spreading lies about me of committing adultery and breaking up his family.

3. Calling up my friends and harassing them and anyone who knows me.

My Strategies

1. Shared dreams and fears.

2. Set rules and boundaries to increase my self-love and self-esteem.

3. Did something new and different.

4. Shielded children from new relationship at early stage.

Could Have Done & Recommendations

1. Notified the police and my lawyers of the abuser's behaviour.

2. Enquire more about John's background to find out if he was married and if there was domestic violence in his family.

CHAPTER SEVEN

Starting A New Life

February 1995, after three months in my temporary shelter, I was offered a three bed flat that I gladly accepted after viewing. It was unfurnished, as my Health Visitor had warned me. Luckily, the Council runs a department with a charity associate where people, especially families in my circumstance, who were unable to furnish their apartments, could apply and get help with used furniture.

When I arrived at the office to apply for what I wanted, it was very confusing. I really couldn't tell what I wanted in my flat, much less say it. The experience was very over-whelming. A nice man was on duty that day. He reminded me of the basic things such as a dining table and chairs, ward-robes, wall divider for the living room and beds because all I mentioned was a settee for the living room. They did not supply electrical goods for health and safety purposes. I was pleased that I did not have to worry about them. I used the money I had saved while in the shelter which was £110 to buy a used gas cooker and refrigerator and voila - our new home was ready.

I was very nervous about moving to the estate because I had not lived in one before. I did not know how to relate to the people there. So I went to the Estate Manager of the Housing Association and asked him the best way to have a peaceful life in such an environment. He told me that to have a peaceful life in such an environment I just had to keep to myself. That was exactly what I did. That piece of advice from the Estate Manager helped me gain respect from the people I lived with.

My Auntie was now able to come and visit me. We began to slowly settle into our new environment. I set some ground rules for the children on relating to other people in the estate and we soon made two good friends and many associates there. I also found a nearby Catholic Church and registered all the children to be baptised. I was so excited to have the opportunity to give the second and third children Christian and meaningful names; as opposed to what Simon registered on their birth certificates. They all got baptised in a little ceremony paid for by my Auntie. She also bought outfits for the children.

We were at the flat for a few months when Simon showed up there one day. The two older children were playing outside when he showed up. They were excited to see him and yet confused when they brought him to my door. They saw shock and fear on my face but didn't understand why. The next question the children asked him after I asked him to leave was, "Daddy, why were you hitting mummy?"

He could not give them any answer. My eldest child was not very keen on Simon. He went with the excitement of his sister the second child. When he left I told the children that I was not happy with Simon showing up and that I was afraid he might harm all of us. I asked them to let me know whenever he showed up at the playground or anywhere in the estate.

Simon kept showing up whenever he pleased. He claimed to want to see the children and brought crisps, biscuits and fizzy drinks. Those were all things I didn't allow the children to have. Each time he showed up the children would become distressed and talk about the violent incidents they had witnessed and this made them unsettled.

I resisted letting Simon come to see the children and got my lawyer involved. My lawyer wrote a letter warning Simon to stay away from me and threatened an injunction against him. I felt used because I was taking care of the children alone while he cruised in to see them and left with nothing more than a visit. He had no feeling of responsibility as a parent. I felt bad because the distress he caused the children each time he showed up affected me and I had to clean up after him. As soon as the children start getting on with their lives, he would show up and disturb the balance. I would be stuck trying to stabilise them again; both emotionally and mentally.

Every time Simon showed up, it brought up bad memories that I was trying to overcome as well. He hadn't changed and still threatened me every chance he could. The fear and bad memories made me sink into depression again and I had to start counselling again for another six weeks. I was getting very tired and decided to request 'respite care' again. That was granted.

My Auntie asked me to let Simon see the children if he wanted. I finally agreed after Simon had pleaded with her. I made him promise not to take the children away or tell them bad things about me. I insisted that he stop threatening me also. I would not allow him access to the children until he agreed to all the conditions. I also told Simon that if he wanted to see the children he has to contribute to their welfare by bringing money for their food, clothing and anything else they needed and may want. I continued by saying that he could not be a father by just buying crisps, biscuits and fizzy drinks whenever he showed up. He needed to know and be concerned with the children being clothed, having food and being warm where they lived. He told me he would not give me any money because I would use the money to look after myself and try to look beautiful for other men so they would admire me. He said he would rather buy what the children wanted but when asked to do that he failed. He later agreed he would give my Auntie £50 every week, which I would have to sign for as proof that he was contributing to the welfare of the children. At first I refused, but later agreed but he never gave my Auntie any money for the children.

When I discovered his pattern of making agreements and never keeping them I decided to stop him from having access to the children completely. I felt he was causing more distress to the children. He would promise to buy them toys and would not show up afterwards or ever purchase them. He would promise to buy them clothes and would not deliver. He would plan a date to come and see them, but would not show up and would not call. He would call me names in front of the children and these upset them. Also, he often told the children I was a prostitute and had slept with an ex-lodger of ours. All these words left the children confused and they always felt lost. Each time I had to pick up the pieces after him.

When I stopped Simon from seeing the children, he started threatening to go to court to exercise his rights to see the children.

Simon had abandoned the children, but I did not want them to feel that way. I never said anything bad about him to the children; I explained to them that violence was wrong and that was why I left their father. I also told them that I wanted to raise them in a happy, loving home and since Simon was not prepared to be part of it, we would have one without him. When they asked if we would live together again, at this time I told them only if their father repents of violence.

Soon after I moved to my flat, John got a job close by. This was nice because he came to see me during lunchtime when he could or he would invite me out for lunch. He was finding it hard settling in his job because he had personality clash with his co-workers who had been at the department longer than him. They were not pleased to see how much attention he was getting. Also, it maybe because he was more qualified than them which resulted in his quick promotion and that made a couple of his colleagues upset. Anyway, John was pleased when I counselled him on how to cope and coached him on how to deal with the issue. He once told me that although I was 25 I reasoned like I was 52. Believe me, at that time I felt like I was 52 because of my workload and the stress I had to cope with. There was this synergy in my relationship with John. I helped him cope with his work and dreams while he helped me relax and encouraged me with my dreams. I was now beginning to let my guards down and had given him a set of keys to my flat so he could let himself in any lunchtime he wanted. He was always welcome to visit if I was not around or if I was having a nap.

I was in my flat for six months now and had dated John for nearly eight months. One day John came over to see me unexpectedly, he said there was something that he had to tell me. That's when he dropped the dreaded news. He told me that he was married with two children and that they were in Africa while he was studying in the UK. He continued by saying that now that he had completed his studies and secured a job his family would be coming to join him in exactly two weeks. Once again, I found myself in shock and feeling deceived. All I could do was exclaim, "What?"

John kept talking and revealed his true age. He was 41 and had a son who was already 19 years old that he had from another relationship, but wasn't particularly close to him. This was a lot for me to take. The first thing I asked after I recovered from the shock enough to speak was, "Is your name really your name?" I went on to ask him if there was anything else he hadn't said that he wanted to tell me. He said that was all.

John was feeling relieved that he had emptied his heart and unburdened his mind. He waited for my response. I was very upset and enquired why he did not tell me about his wife and children when I asked him eight months ago. He told me he did not want to because he never thought our relationship would last this long. He told me his intention was to sleep with me for a while and move on, but as he began to know me it changed. He went on to say that my courage and strength empowered him to overcome any challenges that he was experiencing by seeing how I was able to cope with my challenges and still look after my children. Also, since him getting his job, I had contributed to his success by encouraging him and helping him to cope. Without me, settling at work would have been more difficult.

I gave him a piece of my mind. I called him selfish and told him I felt used. I also informed him that I would not continue with our relationship because I wanted a man of my own and I was not about to cause problems between him and his wife. He said he was sorry and left.

I called my Auntie and my friend Lyn and told them what I had just found out. I cried my heart out and felt so deserted. I was just getting to know John, even love him and then this happened. I felt I could not trust any man again. In fact, I was so hurt from John's news that I decided to put my guards up again and create stricter rules for my relationships. Before dating any man I would know more about him, his family, check out his address and see how easy it was for him to attend to me by visiting me when I wanted. I would even request odd times, perhaps spending the weekend and staying late nights. All these things would help ensure that he wasn't married. This may not have been the cleverest way to ascertain if a man was married or single but it did work for me at that time.

It was a little hard for me to get over John. Each time I remembered the lies, it became easier. I just hated him. That, however, did not stop me from taking him back two months later when he came back and pleaded for me to take him back. He claimed that he was not happy with his wife and that he believed they had grown apart because they had been in separate countries for so long. He believed that his marriage was about to end. I did not believe the B.S; I was more interested in being with him to get over him. That didn't really make sense on the surface, but I felt it would work. In a way, I think I was driven more by hurting him back rather than getting over him.

I gave John tougher conditions and made requests for his time that would hurt his family life. He passed some of these conditions and failed on other ones. Whenever he failed was a good opportunity for me to lash out at him. I felt I had the right to disrespect him for lying to me. But after two or three months I began to feel as if though I was lying to myself. Who was I kidding? I had to tell him to stay away from me for good and move on. I didn't want to admit it, but I knew it to be true. That was what I kept telling myself. I did like having John around for some things though. I kept thinking about how I would miss going out to nice restaurants and clubs. I also liked the money that he gave me sometimes. I'd grown to need it quite badly at different times when money was low and during my Access Course.

* * *

When I started the Access to Sciences Certification Course, which was a requirement for me to obtain advancing to university, I began to feel the pinch for time. I felt I did not have the time to accommodate John in my life now with my children and studies. Besides he had his own family. I had to make a decision and needed a good reason to do that. This was during the two-three month period when I was trying to let John go.

John promised to assist me with childcare costs before I started college. When I started, he paid for the first month but made up an excuse not to pay when the second month childcare cost was due. He stopped returning my calls at that time. When he felt the cost had been paid he showed up and that's when I summoned the courage to tell him to stay away from me for good. I thanked him for the time we had and his support. Then I told him that I wanted more and I deserved more than he could give me. He agreed, but did not understand and still wanted to continue with the relationship. For me that was the end of John. I had bigger dreams and aspirations for myself than to settle as someone's mistress for chicken change. I believed I could earn a lot more money than any man could give me. My financial independence and security were important to me as a woman but my self-respect was even more crucial.

With the new day comes new strength and new thoughts

– Eleanor Roosevelt

CHAPTER LESSONS

Abuser's Controlling Tactics

1. False/empty promises to children.

2. Disruption of children's lives.

3. Distressing the children and I.

4. Showing up at my address unannounced as if it was his right.

My Strategies

1. Asked when unsure.

2. Set rules and boundaries for children.

3. Told children about fear & concerns about ex-abuser.

4. Gave abuser warning letter through lawyer to stay away rather than face him directly.

5. Educated children on domestic violence.

6. Educated children on the best way to handle conflict with family and others without resorting to violence.

7. Cried to let out pain.

8. Got counselling as many times as needed.

9. Got 'respite care' when needed to rest.

10. Started college to work towards financial independence.

Could Have Done & Recommendations

1. Report the distress the abuser caused the children and I to the police.

2. Contact the government or other agencies for help with child care to prevent someone disappointing you and prevent unnecessary financial hardship.

3. Inform my lawyer about the abuser's distress and any financial support arrangement.

4. Go to court to claim financial assistance from the abuser to put a firm arrangement in place.

CHAPTER EIGHT

University Here I Come

The one-year Access Course was fun for me, but hard work. The children and I had to get into a new routine. My new friend and neighbour Kathy, who lived above my flat, would take my first child to play centre while I dropped off the other two at the child minder on my way to college. Kathy would also pick the first child up from play centre and look after him 'til my return. After college I would pick the other two up and get home to make dinner and prepare for the next day.

I had to get all three children ready each morning with this new routine. Luckily, my college was three times a week, but it was still very tiring because of my before and after college activities. There was college course work and studying to do and I was determined to make the grades required to attend my chosen University. Also, I had to pay for childcare for the two younger children from £81 per week I received on Benefits. Eventually, I got help with childcare costs from the government because I was struggling miserably. Cost of running my car, including insurance and occasional repairs were taken care of by Tony and Sue. They had been my friends even since I lived next door to them while I was still with Simon. Bills, clothing, petrol & food all came from £81 per week.

My new neighbours in the Estate were fond of my children and donated clothing to us. We were not close and just said the occasional hello. They were clearly very observant and kind by bringing well-needed items to my door without being asked. I shopped for new clothing from the cheapest high street shops during sales. Other times I picked up clothing from street markets and charity shops. Seeing how much help and support I got from people, even those who hardly knew me really touched me. I wished I could help someone else.

Be careful what you wish for. I'd always heard it and I soon found out why that saying was true. Soon after I prayed and wished for someone to help, my phone rang. An old family friend from Simon's time told me she had left her abusive husband. This came as a complete surprise to me because I did not know she was abused. She heard about my circumstance but had not called me until then. She informed me that she had given birth to her second child and was in hospital but did not have a place to go to because she had fallen out with the friend she was staying with. She wanted a place to stay for three weeks to sort herself out. I was glad to help and picked her up from the hospital the next day. Her first child, who was same age as my first child, joined her in my flat just a few days later.

Since I had three bedrooms, I decided to give them a room. I moved my two children to one room and stayed in one room. My baby, who was just over a year at the time, had to vacate his cot and sleep with me while her baby slept in the cot. Before I knew it, three weeks soon turned into eight months. We all lived on £81 per week of my Benefits and any handouts that came in.

I was glad to have been of help and enjoyed their company. They had to leave a month before I started University to allow me time to settle my children into a new routine and into their room again. Also, I was expecting an Au-Pair (someone to live in with me) named Monica to look after the children while I was at college and needed the room for her.

Meanwhile, Simon still popped in every now and then. It was always just enough to disturb our peace. John still called me, but I chose to disregard their attempts to distract me from my goals. I just wouldn't allow it to happen.

My First Year in University

I started University in October 1996 and was very excited to have reached that stage of my dreams. The course was full-time and intensive. I attended five days a week, 9-5pm each day. On my first week of university my youngest child was admitted into hospital for respiratory problems. It turned out he had a peanut blocking his airways, which had to be removed. He was there for four days and three nights. Right timing; I thought to myself. I had to stop over at the hospital to see him before getting home and had to do my coursework there on one visit. I was getting tired again while the children were trying to get used to Monica.

When the youngest child got back from the hospital I was still struggling to cope with the workload. I commuted to college for an hour each way and had to make dinner too. Of course, I also attended to the children when I got back before they went to sleep. I had to wake up at 3 a.m to check on the children, do my homework or study, go back to sleep at 5 a.m before waking at 6.30am to leave home at 7.30am to university.

After a month of this routine, I knew something had to change. The children were still not as settled as I wanted them to be. I would come home to a distressed Monica who was also eager to get her rest. The children expected me to spend time with them too. University work needed to be done and I needed some rest and time to myself. I was beginning to feel overwhelmed.

One night before I slept, I prayed and poured out my heart to God. I told Him about all my challenges, as if He was not aware of them. I went on to ask him how I could cope and waited for an answer. Being the kind of person I am I wanted an instant answer, but there was none. So I said to God, I'll make a deal with you; I'll look after the children when I am awake and here in the house. While I'm away and at night you look after them and me. I told him that He had to do something and I didn't care how and that was it. I went to sleep feeling very relieved that I could work the day shift and God would work the night shift to look after the children.

I woke at 3 a.m that night and studied for two whole hours without checking on the children. I also went to college that morning without worrying about them or how well they got on with Monica. Since that night, I never had to check on the children at night and whenever any phone calls came for me at the college regarding the children I did not worry. Those calls were few and far in between.

The children soon became settled with Monica. She was very nice and loving. For only being a 19-year-old lady she was just the kind of person I prayed to have. She looked after the children like they were hers. The children respected her like they would me. I told them that she had authority to discipline them like I would. My youngest child was so fond of her that if he woke up at night he crawled into bed with her instead of me. I was not jealous; I was very happy that he felt safe with her. Besides, I had stopped working night shift - remember?

Monica was so nice that she worked longer than she was meant to and did not ask for more money. She also helped me out occasionally on weekends. She was like a younger sister to me and we lived like a family. If she were black, like me, you would not know we were not related but she was from Slovakia.

I obtained a form of government funding called a 'college grant' for my education. That meant that the government paid for my tuition. I could not claim Benefits any longer so I decided to spend £81 per week from the money I got since that was what I was used to spending while on Benefits. I also paid Monica £50 per week, which was the minimum I could pay her. All bills and expenses remained the same, apart from my weekly travel ticket to college.

The money was not enough and I was soon beginning to feel the pinch again. I wanted extra cash but did not know what to do. A friend suggested I take up a Care Assistant job but first I must attend a two-week training course to obtain certification. I decided to do it because I needed to find a way to provide for my family.

During the first holiday in university I enrolled and attended the course for Care Assistant. Soon, I started working as a Care Assistant through an Agency. I got called when someone needed a shift covered. I was only available on weekends. I began working most weekends while attending university weekdays just to have enough cash for my family. My friend Kathy, would look after the children while I was away at work. Sometimes one of the other neighbours would watch the children. Many people were fond of them and kind to offer their help.

Throughout my first year at the university no one in my college knew I had children or about my circumstances. My course mates believed I was like them, but since I lived off campus I couldn't socialise with them often.

I don't believe I missed a single day of college in my first year and I was always on time. The only exception was when there was delay on the transport system. For me, I preferred to attend lectures so I could ask questions if I did not understand. I did not have much time to study on my own and that made me rely mostly on what I gained during lectures for my coursework and exams.

Towards the end of my first year in university I was diagnosed with an overactive thyroid. This simply means that my thyroids were excreting high levels of thyroid hormones. Since the hormones control the rate of the body metabolism it meant my body was working at a faster rate, burning food very quickly and thus making me extremely lethargic. I did not have enough money to eat a lot, and now I was told I should eat more? Where would the money come from? I didn't have the answers. I had to take prescription pills to help stabilise the hormones and was told to get enough rest.

Enough rest? That is what I kept repeating to myself. How could I do that? Couldn't they see I had a goal to achieve? Didn't they see I needed to get a good job to look after my children and myself? How could they not know that I needed a degree from the UK College I was attending? It was a very reputable college and would carry me far if I got deported. That degree could make all the difference. How could they not understand that I had to set high standards for my children? I was their number one role model? Couldn't they see that the society already viewed people who have experienced domestic violence as permanent dependents on the State and lone parents as losers and believe their children would not amount to any good? I couldn't believe they wouldn't know that I was a black woman who was a lone parent raising two black sons. Society already had labelled them as losers and unsuccessful. How could people not know?

I was so determined to give my children the best I could give them. I wanted to remove any stigma society had attached on lone parent families and their children. I wanted to be able to support my children without relying on handouts from the government, friends and neighbours. I wanted to contribute to charity and not remain a charity case for longer than necessary. I had dreams, goals and big visions, but time was not on my side and rest for me was a scarce luxury.

* * *

I believed no one understood what it was like to be me, to have all these big dreams, goals and visions. They couldn't relate to life with all odds against them like they were with me. So now, how would I carry on at the same pace with this diagnosis? I wasn't sure so I did what I've always done. I took it to prayer. For help on setting goals visit www.felicityokolo.com. On the Products page of the website you will find Goal Setting Audio CD. There is also a FREE recording of my interview with Jack Canfield, The Co-Creator of Chicken Soup For The Soul series on Visualisation of your goals and dreams, for you to download on the Free Resource page or you can request a copy of the recording by sending an email to felicity@felicityokolo.com

So I prayed over the diagnosis, took my medication, continued with college and rested when I could. Most of my rest was during the weekend when I went to work. I started work at 1pm and finish at 3 p.m. Then I did another shift from 5 to 7 p.m. In between shifts I would sleep in the car because the distance from where the disabled couples home that I cared for was an hour drive from where I lived and it would be unwise to drive home in between shifts.

My Second Year At The University

Monica stayed with us for 18 months before returning to her country. We missed her so much and we still miss her till today. After her, none of the other Au Pairs lasted more than six months. They certainly didn't care for the children like she did and this posed a challenge for me. By the middle of my second year I was able to get Wednesday afternoons free from my courses. Depending on how I felt that day, I would either stay at the university and study or rush home to catch up with my sleep before the children came home from school. I enjoyed the rest because most of the time neither the Au Pair nor the children knew I was in my room until I emerged all refreshed and excited to see them.

Although I had Wednesday afternoons free, my work-load in college had increased. I was beginning to think that I had bitten off more than I could chew. I also recalled my Health Visitor and some people from my Access Course telling me that it would be best to wait until my youngest child was five years old before attending university. They did not know that I wouldn't have my sanity if I had to wait a day longer than necessary to use my freedom to do what I wanted. As I kept hearing these people's voices ringing in my head about me having bitten off more than I could chew, it began to feel disempowering. It began sending me down to 'Self-pity County' that would soon lead to depression if I let it and I did not like that. I had overcome depression now and literally walking towards the bright light in my life's tunnel. I had to find a way to rise above that feeling and stay focused and true to my dreams and goals.

As usual I found a way to rise above all the chaos in my brain. God was a father to my children and me and He was my first port of call. Then I talked through my challenges with my Auntie and my friends. They encouraged me and promised to continue helping as much as they could. They were all proud of me and believed in me. I viewed their help as an investment in me. This made me want to succeed even more because I wanted to prove to them I was a good invest-ment and wanted them to be very proud of me. This feeling helped me a great deal and kept me going.

During the holidays I made sure I took my children out to a big park for a whole day at least once a week to play with them. Other times they played in the estate or we went to smaller parks. They really cherished those times and still talk about them till this day. I also created 'time with mum-my' once a week. This was where I spent 30 minutes alone with each of the children so they would have my undivided attention and they looked forward to that. My rules for the children remained strict and I committed to a timetable for my schedule. That way I could make life easier for all of us without comprising on fun time. They played out in the playground for 'x' amount of hours then watched TV for 'x' amount of time.

Some people in the Estate looked out for my children while they were at the playground. One day they brought a situation to the attention of the Estate Manager because they considered it a very serious matter. I was not sure who told the Estate Manager, but I was pleased and surprised to see the Estate Manager at my door one late afternoon. He informed me that one of my neighbours had reported that some children at the playground were being racist towards my children. He assured me that he takes racism seriously and I must not tolerate it. He asked me to report any case to him and promised the perpetrators would be dealt with accordingly.

The Estate Manager's visit was a day after my two oldest children came crying to me from the playground. When I enquired why they were crying, they told me that some children called them black. I had raised them to not see people as different and they didn't understand why they were called black. They did not even know their own race. It is not unusual for children under six to not be able to tell the difference in race colour, especially if no one has taught them that. That's what happened with my children.

My children were so saddened and upset by the other children who kept calling them black. I took them inside and comforted them. I then enquired who the children where and they described them. The children they described were the children of another lone parent. I knew how hard it was for me being a lone parent and I did not feel the need to approach the woman. Besides, I believed she got enough confrontation from other parents because her boys were known to be troublemakers.

My children wanted to know if they were black. They looked at their skin tone and told me they couldn't be black because they were brown. I thought about the best way to tell them but only the truth would do. I was forced to explain race, colour and our origin to them. They still did not get why they were called black when their skin tone was brown even after my lecture. I reassured them it was okay to be how they were. Then I made them promise to bring to my attention any such name-calling again. Name-calling hurt them so much because I had raised them not to name-call.

Self Defence

I took up martial arts (Goshin Ju-Jitsu) in college and attended once a week. My main reason for taking these self-defence classes was because of Simon who was still threatening me. I was always out and not physically strong thus, I felt learning some skills in self-defence would be helpful. I ended up liking it as a way to unwind and forgot all about my initial intention. The confidence it gave me whenever Simon was around was enough to scare him and it felt good. There was no need for me to brag or say much. The look I gave him was enough to tell him that he must not mess with me.

By the end of my second year in college my course mates found out I had children. This happened because the children got chicken pox and I missed college for two days. They were all amazed and congratulated me for my courage to take on the challenge of being in the same college as them. They were more motivated to work harder after seeing what I had to cope with. I continued to make the same or better grades than some of them. They also became more helpful. Sometimes I could tell they felt 'sorry' for me, but I did not want that. I hadn't mentioned the children previously for just that reason. I wanted to be treated as 'normal' without the pity element. I did not have the time to wait for their pity; I just got on with what needed doing. I enjoyed receiving more respect from them though.

I missed dating and sometimes I was tempted to date some of the guys that came my way. I tried dating one man briefly and ended it because I wasn't sure he was my type. About six months after dating this man I heard that he had beaten his girlfriend. In turn, he almost got his back broken with a large pestle in self-defence. I found it hard to believe he could be violent, but then again it depends on the woman's rules. If a woman doesn't have the proper rules and boundaries in place then it becomes easier for a man to abuse her. For more information on dealing with domestic violence visit:

www.survivingdomesticviolence.info to download your FREE eBook called Surviving Domestic Violence Info and Tips Booklet or by sending a request by email to felicity@ felicityokolo.com and a copy of the booklet will be sent to you. For Rules, Self-Esteem and Self-Confidence Training visit: www.felicityokolo.com for details on the Training page or email felicity@felicityokolo.com to be sent the details.

I received Access Funding in addition to my 'college grant' and took out student loans, which needed my immigration documents to be presented. Somehow I was still granted the loan without the immigration documents. My immigration status had been making me weary. It was still in limbo and because I knew Simon wanted me deported, I decided to sort out my immigration myself by getting a new lawyer that Sue recommended. When I approached the previous lawyer handling my case, who was acting under Simon's direction, he refused to attend to me or hand me any document, not even my passport. It took several months of endless phone calls and tears before I summoned up the courage to attend his office for the third time and told his PA that I will not leave the office without my passport and letters from the Home Office regarding my case. I was yelling when he came out and called me into his office. It was then he told me that Simon warned him not to communicate with me or give me any of the Home Office documents apart from my passport. I demanded to have a copy of my marriage Affidavit that proved I was legally married to Simon. He refused because Simon forbade him from doing so because he was paying him. I refused to leave his office until he got Simon on the phone. He took the call in his PA's office so I would not listen in.

When he returned to his office he told me that I could have the marriage Affidavit, but it had been misplaced. He asked me to come back in a few days to pick it up. I went back a week later, my earliest convenient time and picked up the document. I passed the Affidavit, along with my passport onto my new lawyer. Months that seemed like years went by and I heard nothing from the Home Office. The UK immigration Law was fast changing and it was a matter of time before I was found out and probably deported. One such incident was when an Au Pair I invited was stopped at the airport. The immigration office called me and wanted to know my immigration status to know if I had rights to invite someone into the country. After a ten-minute interview on the phone they were not satisfied. They spoke with the agency I got the Au Pair from and called me back for another ten minutes. By God, I could not remember what they asked and what answer I gave to them. The Au Pair was refused entry. I kept worrying that the immigration office would show up anytime and deport us. I had to wait another week for a new Au Pair.

It took about 18 months from the date of my encounter with the immigration officers regarding the Au-Pair case for my immigration fears to hit me head on. I was so scared.

Immigration Officers Visit

One Sunday morning at 8 a.m., while I was in my final year in college (May 1999) and close to completion, I heard a hard firm knock on my door. I was still sleeping and had another hour to rest before getting ready for church. I was almost upset to be woken up by that loud knock and was determined to tell whoever it was off. I heard the knock even louder the second time and jumped out of bed, put on my dressing gown, rushed to the front door and looking through the spy hole I enquired who it was. A voice from the other side replied, "Immigration." From the spy hole on the door I could see a man and woman standing there. They both looked very serious and the man was carrying a huge pile of papers. All I could do was say, "Hold on." The panic started and I did not know what to do or what to say. I hurried into the living room, grabbed the codeless phone and quickly called my Auntie. I rushed into the toilet because I was almost pissing on myself by this time. As the immigration officers continued to knock I quickly told my Auntie what was happening and told her if she doesn't hear from me after an hour she should know we have been deported.

With that said I rushed to the door and let the officers in. I apologised for the delay in letting them in. We stood in the hallway while they asked me to identify myself, which I did. They asked me the number of people in the flat, I told them my three children and I. They looked at me suspiciously and asked me that same question again and I answered the same. They then enquired about my Au Pair as the fifth person in the flat. I informed them I had an Au Pair, but did not view her as my family and that was reason why I did not count her.

They asked me to show them round the flat. I showed them the storeroom, the bathroom, the toilet, the kitchen and then the living room. I warned them the children were in there before showing them. I continued and showed them the children's room and pointed to the room where the Au Pair was and told them she was asleep and I didn't want to disturb her. They didn't mind not seeing the room.

After giving them a tour of the flat their tone of voice was a little calmer. I invited them into my bedroom to talk more because I did not want to disturb or alarm the children in the living room watching TV. While in my bedroom they told me the purpose of their visit. They informed me while looking at my huge file, which they'd had with them for a long time that they wanted to come and see for themselves what was happening. I explained to them that I was not re-ceiving Benefits and would be completing my degree in a month's time, after which I would be getting a job so I could fend for my children and me. They enquired about Simon and I told them he lived on his own in our previous address. They gave me their names and office address and said to me that if I wanted to contact them for anything I should feel free to do so.

When they left, I was so relieved and could not believe I was still in the country. I quickly called my Auntie and shared the news with her. I cried out of relief before getting the children ready for church. The next day I called my lawyer and informed him of the immigration visit to my address. He assured me that everything would work out well soon. A month after the immigration visit to my place, I completed my degree in Microbiology with Honours.

The following month I got a contract job in the outskirts of London. It was for three months initially. It was an hour drive away and the money was not great but I took it just to gain experience. A month after starting my new job I wanted extra money and so I started applying for higher paying jobs while waiting for my contract to end. My friend Kathy had heard me complain about wanting extra money. She told me she could help me get a part-time job where she worked. At first I hesitated, but later I decided to try it out.

At the time, Kathy worked as a cleaner in a bank close to our Estate. She worked two hours in the morning and two hours in the evening. She had a husband who had a small restaurant and a son same age as my first child. I didn't think she was desperate for money, but she did it to have some income of her own while she learned English. I've heard about and seen many people talk about cleaning jobs. Some people assumed that was all they could get for income, but that had never been me.

I told Kathy I would try it out for a month just for the experience of seeing what it felt like working as the lowest part in a company hierarchy. The job paid about £3-4 per hour, as of then. I started going for just the morning and cleaned with Kathy. I would come home, have a quick bath and go to my main job. This meant I had to wake up at 4 am. After a week I felt sick of the job. We were paid fortnightly and I had to stick around for another week before being paid.

After the second week at the cleaning job I began to feel sorry for people whom I met there. Some of them depended on the job and had to tolerate bullying and insults from the supervisors. Plus, the bank workers who came really early sometimes looked down on them. I knew I was there for the experience of doing a cleaning job and so my confidence was much higher than most people I met there. Although none of them knew anything about me, I listened more to their stories when I could. There wasn't much time for stories because of how quickly you had to work in a short amount of time. I thought that the work required more than two hours to complete. I truly believe the cleaners were overworked, underpaid and not respected for their role.

I completed my experiment of working as a cleaner in a bank for a month. I cleaned toilets for that entire month. I vowed NEVER to do such a thing again or to let any circumstance occur that may force me to EVER do it again.

I continued with my main job until the end of my contract. I did not want my contract renewed because I was not challenged in the job. This was the case even though it was work in my field of study; I felt it was not a graduate role. While waiting to get another job we had to move because our block of flats in the Estate needed to be demolished to make way for a new development.

I continued on.

It is interesting to notice how some minds seem almost to create themselves, springing up under every disadvantage, and working their solitary but irresistible way through a thousand obstacles.

– Washington Irving

CHAPTER LESSONS

Abuser's Controlling Tactics

1. Refused to allow our lawyer to hand over my immigration documents.

2. Popped in whenever to disturb our peace.

My Strategies

1. Got friends to help drop off and pick up children from school.

2. Got help with childcare cost from government.

3. Shopped at cheapest high street shops, street markets and charity shops.

4. Offered help to a friend in similar situation without caring if we had enough or not.

5. Had plenty of time to settle children and myself into new routine.

6. Got live-in child helper for convenience.

7. Asked for Divine help to resolve challenges.

8. Got government funding for education.

9. Took on part-time job to help with cash flow.

10. Held on to dreams & goals no matter what.

11. Talked to trusted friends & families about challenges.

12. Created quality time for each child.

13. Set moral and ethical rules for children.

14. Raised children under six not to know race colour.

15. Took self-defence classes not just to defend myself, but also for self-confidence.

16. Did what needed to be done without worrying about "the system". I just kept believing.

17. Shared joy and sorrows with friends and family.

18. Tried something new, but did not like it and vowed to never let myself get into such situation again.

Could Have Done & Recommendations

1. Get a new immigration lawyer once separated from the abuser.

PART THREE

The man of virtue makes the difficulty to be overcome his first business, and success only a subsequent consideration.

– Confucius

CHAPTER NINE

Out With The Old And In With The New

In January 2000, we moved into our new home. A three-bed terraced house with front and back gardens. It was very nice. For our new home, I decided it was time to buy new things. After living for five years with second hand furniture and charity items I wanted something different. Now I was a graduate, just got a new job, was no longer on government Benefit; I just had to upgrade.

We took nothing from our old flat except my bed, which I loved, our clothing and any personal belongings plus the cooker. I bought a new settee for our living room, a new dining table and chairs, new washing machine, new beds for the children and our wardrobes were purchased a couple of months later, along with a new cooker. It felt good to have all new things in the house and kitchen utensils that were colour coordinated with the kitchen décor. The house was decorated with our desired wallpapers and paint.

I felt kind of proud of myself for my achievements and I believed the children were proud of me too. This really showed when people visited. It was nice to see how flabbergasted they were to see the photo of me graduating from Imperial College that hung on the wall of my living room.

The Au pair I had at that time was no longer needed because my eldest child was almost nine, the second was seven and half, and the youngest was five and half. Their new school was literally a two minutes walk away from our new home. The next month was spent establishing a new routine for the children without an Au Pair and without me. I taught the children how to do things for themselves, such as using the washing machine and ironing their clothes, so they would become independent. That way I could use my spare energy to play with them. I explained to them that I had to work to earn money so I could take care of us. I reminded them that I loved them and wanted them to be successful and independent and reason why it was good for them to learn to do things for themselves and help out whatever way they could for their respective ages. We made friends very quickly at the new Estate and the children settled quickly. The children went to school by themselves and came home by 4 p.m. They would start on their homework, except for the youngest one who attended an after school club that closed at 6 p.m. I got back just before 6 p.m to pick him up. Sometimes a neighbour or friend would pick him up if I was delayed by traffic. We all made and ate dinner together in the kitchen-diner. Afterwards, I would check on their homework and find out about their day. By the time that was all done, it was already bedtime.

I usually called the house just after 4 p.m. to make sure the other two children were home and getting on with their homework. I also had a neighbour who checked on them to make sure they were fine. With my new job, I worked only weekdays and had weekends to rest and spend quality time with the children. Things were really looking up and I was so happy.

When I completed my degree program I decided to stop my thyroid medication and started resting more. I had to check the hormone levels with my doctor every couple of months or if I felt really weak just to make sure it was safe for me to stay off the pills.

The move had also brought peace of mind in regards to Simon. I was glad to be away from the address he knew. Although I knew he would soon find me, I was more than willing to have a few months of peace without him. As always, when he showed his ugly face it distressed the children. Then I was always left to do damage control.

Like most people who have immigration problems, I was glad that I had moved to a new address that the immigration officers did not know. Since I didn't leave any forwarding address for my mails, I believed they would not find me easily. Believe me, at the time I thought and felt I was in the right and so clever. Now that I am writing this, I can't help but laugh at myself on how stupid I was for thinking I was being clever. How could I move literally twenty minutes from my previous address and in the same country with a car, job and children and think that immigration would not find me if they wanted to? Anyway, since their last visit in

May 1999 I had not heard from them and I believed it was good to let sleeping dogs lie.

Simon soon found us and as usual, the children came home crying. My second child; my daughter was particularly upset. Maybe it's the father/daughter connection that upset her, but it was clear that Simon was not being genuine. His intention has always been to bring me down and to see me unhappy. He didn't care who or what he used to get to me. Now, he was slowly working away at my daughter to get me.

I had promised myself not to say anything bad about him, but I sure was tempted to do it several times. I had to find a way to help the children see he did not have good intentions and he really did not want to see them. I contacted my lawyer, who wrote to him to stop coming to our Estate. He then decided to get his lawyers on my case again using his 'god' - the barrister - who advised him to marry someone and have children just to save his property.

Simon claimed he wanted to see the children and promised to contribute to their welfare. Again, he wanted to drop off £50 per week at my Auntie and then I must sign for. Even when I agreed to his terms, he never fulfilled them; not even once. He also claimed he was sorry and that he wanted me back. We agreed to attend mediation to save on cost of going to court to see if we can come to an agreement on how he could see the children regularly and contribute to their welfare. A welfare officer made this agreement after several meetings and interviews with him, the children and me separately.

The Mediation

The first mediation session, probably February or March 2000 with Simon made me sick. I was sick at the sight of him sitting opposite me. The mediation centre was on alert to call the police if he tried to get violent. I was so consumed with my emotions that I did not remember I had martial arts training. I relied on the police being called if Simon were to get violent. This was the first opportunity Simon had gotten since I left him in 1994 to sit in my presence for one whole hour and insult me. It was a disaster, he was well prepared and I wasn't. All he did was say all kinds of derogatory things about me; how I was a bad mother, a prostitute, how he had more money than me and could take care of the children better than me. I kept bringing the discussion back to the main point, which was the best way forward about the children, but he was more interested in putting me down. The session coordinator found it hard to control him until I threatened to leave if Simon didn't keep quiet and allow me to speak. He still didn't stay silent for long.

At the end of the session, I had to leave twenty minutes before him. That way he would not have an opportunity to attack me. I went home feeling so down and cried my eyes out. The way Simon spoke, with such hatred, would make one think he spoke about something that just happened the night before, but it was six years ago.

When I told my friends about what happened they were upset because I was upset. Since Simon started stressing the children and I after I left him, I wanted him dead. I wished and prayed he would just drop dead. I even told him at the session that he should do everyone a favour and just die because he was of no use. With the recent happenings I wished he would die very quickly and leave the children and me in peace. I had left his 'precious' house; the Child Support Agency had been trying for six years to get money off him for the children and had been unsuccessful and he was not about to give me any money to support the children.

Simon was even bitterer that I had not apologised to him for sleeping with an ex-lodger and for leaving him. He felt I was adding insult to injury by preventing him from seeing his children. Which children I asked? Did he mean the youngest one? That was the child he claimed was not his. Perhaps he meant all three since he had them just to save his property.

I became desperate. On this ground, I wanted to leave the country and go very far away from him where he would not find us. I continued applying for the American Visa lottery I had been applying for the past two years with hopes that my degree would make a difference to the application.

The next mediation session was just two weeks away. I told the counsellor I would not attend unless Simon refrained from insulting me and promised to focus on the main point of the programme. Simon agreed and the next session was booked. During the session Simon did not just insult me. He also went at my parents and my whole family. After about half an hour of listening to Simon B.S I got up and left the room. That was the end of the mediation session. I refused to attend any more sessions because Simon uses it to put me down and I knew I was too good to give him my time and receive insults in return. I gave him a single condition. If he was serious about seeing the children he must learn to behave. With regards to me getting back with him he could kiss my ass because the answer is NEVER. I had moved on and he had remained where he was and probably even more dangerous than he was when I was with him.

His lawyer wrote on his behalf threatening to go to court if I would not attend mediation to resolve the matter and allow him to see the children. Apart from the fact that he used the children to get to me, I did have a genuine fear about Simon abducting the children or killing them just to hurt me. This was all happening at the time when a man had killed his three children when he picked them up from his ex-wife for visit. The man fed the children drugged food and connected the exhaust fumes of his car to the inside with all three children sleeping in the car. There were also two cases at the same time where two abusive husbands killed their ex-wives at police stations. All this scared me and I tried to protect my children even more. I had worked hard to raise them to this age. The thought of someone taking their lives now or hurting them in any way was enough to send me to my grave. This made me not be afraid of Simon or his lawyer's threats because my children's safety was paramount.

Simon took me to court. He claimed he wanted to see the children because he loved them. Love? What? Simon would not recognise love if it hit him in the face. What does he know about love I thought to myself? The only things he 'loves' are his properties and other possessions.

We lived on.

If I had a formula for bypassing trouble, I would not pass it round. Trouble creates a capacity to handle it. I don't embrace trouble; that's as bad as treating it as an enemy. But I do say meet it as a friend, for you'll see a lot of it and had better be on speaking terms with it.

– Oliver Wendell Holmes

CHAPTER LESSONS

Abuser's Controlling Tactics

1. False promises and arrangements.

2. Distressing the children and me.

3. Showing up in my new address whenever he felt like it.

4. Threat to go to court to exercise his rights

My Strategies

1. Praised myself and recognised my achievements.

2. Established routine to meet new changes.

3. Got children to help prepare meals and ate together afterwards.

4. Taught children to do things for themselves for independence and also to avoid being a slave instead of a mum.

5. Played with children.

6. Told children reason why they had to help out and reminded them they are loved.

7. Made children understand why I had to work.

8. Resisted temptation of saying derogatory things about the abuser to the children.

9. Made sure mediation was in a safe centre.

10. Refused to accept or believe empty promises, agreements and pleas from abuser when action did not reflect his words.

11. Children's safety and welfare were paramount.

Could Have Done & Recommendations

1. Not give abuser opportunity to see me one-to-one.

2. Not attend the second mediation session after the insults from the first one.

CHAPTER TEN

Switch

My current job this time was also in the outskirts of London and the daily drive, which was the cheapest travel option, was beginning to take a toll on me. I started hunting for jobs in London. Most jobs needed at least one year experience and I did not have that yet. I soon began to lose interest in my field. Most companies that wanted me were out of London and that was not good enough; especially when I recalled a time I fell asleep behind the wheels on the motorway due to exhaustion while on my way back home from work.

I decided to switch careers because this was the height of the IT (Information Technology) boom. A friend of mine who helped me with my computer problems suggested it would be a good idea to do an IT course and get a job in London. I thought about it and agreed to go with his suggestion. The cost of the course, which he recommended; MCSE (Microsoft Certified System Engineer) was about £4000 at that time which was quite high for me. Luckily the government offered subsidy for the course.

One day, this friend called me and told me he saw an advertisement about a college offering the course for £999 with the government covering the rest of the fees; plus you got a free computer. I called up the college the next day and went to see them. Everything the Ad said was right, but for me to qualify for government subsidy I must show I was legally entitled to it. This referred back to my immigration status. I was disappointed and felt bad.

After two days of sulking and thinking of what to do, I called my lawyer and asked him to contact the Home Office to ask them to speed up my case. I was no longer afraid for some strange reason. I guess each time my survival was threatened, all fears seem to disappear. My lawyer called me back two days later to say that the Home Office just informed him that they wrote to me six months ago that the matter has been resolved, but the letter was sent back to them saying the addressee no longer resided there. He requested the letter be sent to him instead which he then forwarded unto me by recorded delivery.

* * *

It was now October 2000 and it turned out the Home Office wrote me in April informing me that my children and I could remain indefinitely in the UK and we had all rights to claim all a UK citizen could claim. Now who is the clever one I asked myself? There I was hiding from the Home Office and losing out on what I so desired.

I was so happy and relieved to receive that letter. I think I celebrated for a whole month; especially knowing for certain now that Simon could never have me deported. What about Simon, I wondered? I later found out his case was ignored at that time while mine was successful. The day after I received the letter I rushed to the college and enrolled for the course. I paid £200 deposit and set up a payment plan to cover the balance of £799. The government covered the rest of the £4000 tuition. The course was for a year. I felt I didn't have one year and wanted to complete it sooner so I could secure a job in London. I figured out a way and completed the course in five months. I had to quit my job and studied it full-time.

* * *

A couple of months after completing the course I got a job in central London which was good and I was very pleased because the company I worked for was just two train stops from where l lived. It took me 15-20 minutes to get to work.

Meanwhile, when Simon took me court, I decided to file for divorce since my immigration status had been resolved. The courts granted Simon visitation rights for two hours every fortnight at a 'contact centre' where the visit would be supervised. These centres were also on neutral grounds and the 'contact visits' were pending review subject to Simon's behaviour. One of my conditions for the children attending the 'contact centre' was for a taxi to take us there and take us back home afterwards. Simon must pay for it because it would be unethical to ask me to pay for our travel to the centre; especially when it was for Simon's benefit and because Simon refused to give any money directly to me for the travel cost. So every fortnight, Simon would pay my local taxi firm and they would pick us up to go to the 'contact centre.' I waited in the waiting area while contact took place. Then I took the children home in the taxi afterwards.

Simon would buy snacks and fizzy drinks for the children. Occasionally he would give them £5 each or give £20 to my daughter alone; whom he claimed gave him the most attention. This would make the boys jealous, but he did not care. Eventually I complained about it to my lawyers and they threatened to stop contact if Simon didn't start treating the children fairly.

My eldest and youngest children did not like going to see him; especially the first child because of the memories of the abuse he had witnessed. Almost every time he saw Simon he asked him why he hit mummy. He promises to buy them things, which he sometimes did and at other times he would make up excuses why he didn't.

* * *

A few months after getting my new IT job I bought a fairly new car, took the children for summer holiday to Nigeria to see their grandparents, and the rest of my family. They returned to London with my mother who replaced me at the 'contact centre' visit so I could avoid seeing Simon.

After about six months of using the 'contact centre' to see the children Simon went back to ask the court for review. He wanted the children to visit him at his house. To put my mind at peace from fear of abduction, the court asked him to surrender his passport to my lawyers and sent alert letters to the immigration and passport offices. These letters would forbid them from processing any passport application for the children that Simon might make. They also prevented him from taking the children out of the country without my permission. As for killing them, all I had was my belief and trust in God. I told the children what the court order was and taught them how to defend themselves, how to get back home on their own, how to reverse call me on my mobile number (which I made sure they knew by heart) and how to get help if and when the need arose while with Simon. I also taught them acceptable and not acceptable behaviour between adults and children. I wanted them to know everything possible to help prevent them being abused.

The first visit to Simon's house didn't have a good start. He had to pick them up at 11 a.m. just after church. He was supposed to pick them up at my Estate at a pickup point few yards from my house because I didn't want him to see me. He was to bring the children back by 7 p.m. on Sundays every fortnight so they could prepare for school the next day. He was supposed to feed them lunch and dinner.

Simon was half an hour late getting there and then he returned the children half an hour late. He fed them junk food and they brought part of it home. Even worse than junk food was the emotional and mental food he fed them. He referred to me as a prostitute while talking to the children. He told them I slept with men to feed them. He told them I had no money and that they should come and live with him because he had more money than me and he had two properties and I didn't have any.

I was glad to see them back home safe and well but I could not get away from their persistent question why Simon referred to me as a prostitute. I had to tell them the story I believe Simon holds on to about me sleeping with an ex-lodger. About me sleeping with men to feed them, I told them I was dating a man because I loved him and I had a job to support them. What if I had to sleep with a man to support the children I thought to myself, wouldn't that be a shame on Simon? How would he feel knowing that is how his children got fed? But then again, it would not matter to him because he didn't care and it wasn't about the children. It was all about him and his attempts to destroy my life for leaving him.

After about three visits to his house I felt the children were safe and decided to use the time while they were with Simon to have a nap or go out with friends. Simon continued to use the children visits to dump his BS onto them instead of building relationships with them. Again, he made promises that he didn't keep and since there was no one to supervise it was his word against the children's. Once he had promised to buy the children saxophones. This got them all excited. They came back after one visit with toy saxophones that made so much noise and drove me mad.

All three children attended Saturday music and drama classes at the time. The eldest wanted a proper saxophone, not toy saxophone. He was very disappointed and cried when he got home when all he got was a toy saxophone. When he told Simon at the next visit he wanted a proper saxophone Simon said he did not have the money to buy it. When he confronted Simon about the money he bragged about, Simon threatened him and yelled at him. Since then, my eldest hated going to visit Simon. The empty promises and the names Simon called me were too much for him to bear. I explained to him that it was courts order that he goes, but if he wasn't happy I would speak to my lawyer about it, and I did.

Simon was warned that if he did not stop distressing the children during visitation the order would be withdrawn. Besides, he missed picking them up every now and then without notice. That kept the children waiting and it ruined every ones plans for that day.

The visitation order was later withdrawn because Simon just could not help himself. Simon went back to court to appeal against the order and stated he wanted visitation rights to be extended to weekend stays. I contested his application on grounds of him causing distress to the children. By now I had the 'contact' and divorce case going on at the same time.

I had to pay £133 per month towards my court fees. Simon got all his costs paid for by the Legal Services Commission (LSC). I was very upset and gave the LSC all the information I knew about Simon's earnings and properties.

Yet, he still paid nothing towards his court fees. I couldn't help but feel that I was being treated unfairly and was let down by the system. How hard was it for the system to know that based on my salary at that time, which was £17,500 per annum, I was not a wealthy woman? I had three children to look after, plus bills and other expenses. Simon had lodgers in two properties, no dependants, and earned probably three times what I earned from his taxi business. He got to pay nothing? It was very wrong.

Since Simon paid nothing towards his court fees, he did not care how long the case lasted. I wanted a quick end to the case without compromising on my children's happiness. The money I was paying to go to court was cutting deep into our living expenses so I had to take up a Care Assistant job one hour in the evenings after my main job to earn extra money to meet the court costs. I was now attending court at least once a month and had to take time off work on the day.

I was under enormous financial and emotional stress again. My thyroid started acting up again and I now suffered from migraines on a regular basis. The visitation order was re-instated while the divorce case and weekend stay cases continued.

My work was suffering and I was taking more time off work for illness than usual and the company directors did not like it. I explained to them my circumstance and hoped they understood. One day at work, two weeks before Christmas of 2002, my migraine was so bad. I tried to brave it because I did not want to take time off work for illness again. After about an hour I could not bear the pain anymore. I stood up and started walking over to my line manager to tell her I was ill. The next thing I knew, I heard voices and saw myself on the floor with paramedics around me. Apparently, I had fallen and passed out. While still in the 'recovery position' the paramedics continued checking for my speech, vision and touch. Just then, I saw two pairs of legs stepping over me. They were those of the CEO and CTO (Chief Technical Officer) of the company. I watched them literally step over me without stopping to enquire what was happening. I was taken to hospital accompanied by a colleague from work. I spent about six hours in accident and emergency for observation. The doctors couldn't find out what was wrong with me. They ended up giving me stronger painkillers and sent me home. The next day my line manager called and informed me that the CTO said I should take the rest of the year off to recover.

* * *

In January 2003 I went back to work and still had the court case. Luckily a doctor from my General Practitioner Surgery found out I had blocked sinuses and once that was cleared I was much better. The migraines soon disappeared, but the financial and emotional stress continued because of the court cases and concerns about the distress Simon caused the children.

Losing My Ideal Job

In February 2003, Simon was granted the right to take the children for weekend stays every fortnight. That same month I was fired from my job. They claimed I had not been performing well and had another job that was taking my focus away from my main job. I was very upset. I thought they understood my circumstances. I had explained to the CTO about why I needed a second job and he actually gave me a reference before I started the job. Why fire me now?

I blamed Simon for losing my job. I had worked so hard to get to where I was. I had a good paying job close to my home and now this happened. I had a car to pay for and other financial commitments that Benefits will not cover. I did not know what to do. I decided to stay off work until the court cases were over. Two months later, the cases were over and Simon celebrated victory and also stopped picking up the children for fortnightly visits. He never once took the children for a weekend stay till this day.

I was so annoyed at his stupidity, or should I say, his wickedness. What benefit was there in dragging me through the courts to get the order and not use it? I came to the conclusion that Simon was just out to get me. He loved to win cases and it did not matter who got hurt. He wanted to see me down and to remain down. This made him happy. Based on his refusal to take the children for the weekend stays that he was granted and his role in getting me stressed out to the point of losing my job, I decided to stop him from having any form of contact with the children.

I was mad and did not care what the court order said. I felt I had been treated unfairly and lost my job in the process. It was all for nothing and I was still counselling the children on how to get over Simon's distress.

I was glad to finally get my divorce granted. However, I did not get my £30,000 divorce settlement because it went back to the LSC for lawyers costs. It seemed I definitely lost everything, but my children's happiness.

We lived on.

Look not mournfully into the past, it comes not back again. Wisely improve the present, it is thine. Go forth to meet the shadowy future without fear and with a manly heart.

– Henry Wadsworth Longfellow

CHAPTER LESSONS

Abuser's Controlling Tactics

1. Distressing the children while with him.

2. Attempt to disrupt children's routine.

3. Attempt to destroy the children's confidence in me - their mother.

My Strategies

1. Changed careers when not challenged and for safety reasons.

2. Used self-made Fast Track to complete course when not happy with the 'normal' setup.

3. Made abuser pay for cost of travel to 'contact centre' that was supervised.

4. Avoided direct contact with abuser.

5. Made abuser surrender travel documents through lawyer for fear of children being abducted.

6. Got children to memorise mobile number for emergencies.

7. Taught children how to be safe while with abuser.

8. Got lawyer to warn abuser to stop distressing children or visits may stop.

9. Counselled children on how to deal with abuser derogatory behaviours.

Could Have Done & Recommendations

1. Get professional help for the children to cope with the abuser's distress and disruptions.

ll

Taking Time To Reflect

I decided to take a year break from work. I was disappointed with the LSC procedure of awarding government legal funding. I was disappointed with my employer's lack of understanding of my circumstance. Even more disappointed that the company CEO and CTO stepped over me to get to their desks without caring. Only the CTO enquired about my health two weeks after the incident when I returned to work. The CEO of the company, who was a woman, did not show any human compassion.

Those reasons lead to me vowing to never work for anyone again. I took a year to explore my options. As the saying goes, "When life gives you lemons, make lemonade". I felt it was just the right time to get the well-needed rest doctors have always told me I needed. Come to think of it, throughout the four and half years I spent with Simon, I was either pregnant or nursing a baby. Then the next four years I was a student and was working full-time for the next three years.

My year off of work turned out to be the most fun year I had spent with my children. I told them I was available 24/7 for them. I went to school day trips with them when they wanted me to. I attended all school plays, sports events, parents meetings and did whatever they wanted me to do. I was able to take them to weekday curricula activities as well; plus, the weekend one they attended. I slept until I could sleep no more. I even put on weight to my amazement and to that of my friends who truly believed I was born to be a size 10, but I was now a size 12.

Since I didn't have the stress of going to court my thyroid was now normal again. Also I believe that with no job and no college to attend my body was free to relax more and function at its utmost. Six months into my year out, even with all the fun and rest, I was getting a little bored. Since I had promised the children I was taking the year out, I had to keep to my promise. With a career in IT I felt the industry was fast paced and I was concerned I might get behind. Instead of feeling left behind I decide to attend a 12-week part-time Web-Design course. I attended that once a week. The children's approval was important to me or else I would feel guilty for breaking my promise. Even with the course they knew if they needed me on the day of the course I would attend to them because I did the course just to have something less tasking to do while I rested.

After my year out, I started my own home business so I could work flexible hours. That would allow me to spend time with the children and prevent what I had experienced in my previous role as an employee.

Meanwhile Simon phoned or texted me whenever he felt like releasing BS from his mouth. He started threatening me again for preventing him from seeing the children because he refused to follow court orders. My two sons were very disturbed with his behaviour and they also claimed he scares them. They did not want to see him. Their feelings were strongly enforced from all the promises that he never delivered on too.

* * *

When he promised to buy a saxophone and failed I had to spend about £600 on a saxophone. When he promised to buy a keyboard and failed I had to spend about £150 on a keyboard. These expenses were difficult because I also had clothing and other things to purchase for the household. The children began to question him about the money he claimed to have. They asked him why he wouldn't buy what he promised if he had so much money. His answers were that he had mortgages to pay, or he would tell them that he would pay 1/3 towards the cost of the item while I paid the balance. Every time I agreed to such arrangements he still did not deliver. He told the children that if they wanted him to pay for things they needed they must come and live with him. I told the children that they could go and live with him when they are older if they wanted, but for now he could start taking them for weekends first and we would see how that worked out before moving on to the next step.

Conquering Domestic Violence

While still on my year break and with time on my hands I decided to think, evaluate the situation and take time to reflect on my life and Simon's behaviours. I thought hard about Simon's motivation; why he did what he did, why he was the way he was, and why he did not care about his children. I figured out he was the way he was because that is the only way he knew how to be. He did not know any different, so how could he behave differently? He didn't what to learn how to be a better parent or better person so why should I bother with him? It could be that he was happy with the way he was.

I decided it was time to put him behind me forever. To do that I had to forgive him for all the pain he caused me. I had to release all the bitterness I felt towards him. I had to stop wishing him death. It was not easy but it had to be done. I forgave him without him apologising because he wouldn't apologise even if his life depended on it. I had to forgive him for my sake. I prayed to God to give him love and happiness, whatever that meant to him. I said this prayer not just for his benefit, but also for the sake of the children and me, for us to have peace. I believed that if he had some love and happiness in his life, he would not have much time to bother us. I stopped wishing he would die because it is best he lives to see what the children he didn't love or care for become in the future. I believed that would be the greatest victory for me. I also told him he could see the children when he wanted if they wanted to see him and they could stay over if they wanted to. I also had to forgive myself for tolerating the

abuse for the period I was with Simon because every now
and then I blame myself for staying, for trying to be a good
girl to my parents by marrying him and for being stupid by
thinking the abuse will stop.

The children were not afraid to challenge him by now.
When he said anything profane or derogatory about me they
would argue with him about it. The fact that he was not con-
sistent in any arrangements he made and didn't keep most
of his promises did not help him either. I was always there to
comfort the children at the end of the day and remind them
they did not have to do anything they did not want to do.

At this time I felt I was ready to start a relationship that
would lead to marriage. I felt the children were old enough
and had plenty of my undivided attention for some time.
This was especially true in the early to primary school stage
of their lives. I had never wanted them to have any competi-
tion. As usual, I put out there the type of man I wanted and
worked to be the kind of woman for that kind of man.

Of all three children, my daughter was the most tempted
of Simon's promises and bravado about money. She wanted
a piece of that. Simon focused on her. He called her and
came over to deliver the odd £10 or £20 to her and gave
nothing to her brothers. Sometimes she would confront him
about neglecting her brothers and this would make him give
them some money. She would go and visit him whenever he
wanted and when she wanted. She felt it was the perfect rosy
life to have two homes. He kept tempting her to come and
live with him so he would give her more. She became unruly
because she felt 'daddy' had a room for her and would let

her do whatever she wanted there. He seemed to be willing to give her whatever she wanted, even if it was bad for her or not appropriate for her age. I would not tolerate that.

For that reason she decided to go and live with him. I was scared for her safety because Simon had other plans. Her brothers, my new partner, and I were all hurt. Simon was hardly around. He worked 7 days and probably 7 nights as a mini-cab (taxi) driver and was hardly around to be a parent.

I later found out after about a month of my daughter moving in with him that he was treating her like he treated me. He refused to buy food if she was unruly. He started hitting her first with his bare hands. He hit and punched her. This progressed to him using slippers to beat her, then a tree branch, not a twig but a branch from the back garden, my daughter told me. It then progressed even further. He beat her with a cord that had metal in the middle. He would beat her and sometimes while she was crying he would start crying and blame her for making him beat her. He claimed seeing her cry reminded him of himself when his father used to brutally beat him. When his father was not around and he was unruly, his mother would ask his elder brother to beat him up.

I recalled Simon telling me once while we were together that the brutal beatings from his father and elder brother were so bad and continued into his teens. Then he became strong enough to fight off and beat his father. Once he could do that the abuse stopped.

Initially my daughter lied about the bruises I saw on her when she came to visit me. She covered up for him and didn't want to acknowledge that staying with him was a wrong decision. I confronted her one time when I suspected Simon was beating her. She confessed that he hit her once without mentioning other incidents. I reminded her, as I'd always done, the reason why I left Simon. I told her that he was not ready to change and not even she could make him change unless he wanted to. I went on to tell her that I did not want her and her brothers to experience abuse from Simon and that's why I took them away from the environment. I added that if she enjoyed being abused then it was up to her. That was so difficult.

The next time Simon tried to hit her she fought him off and ran out of the house. He had to beg her to come back and promised not to hit her. By this time she did not believe him anymore, but she felt sorry for him because he was alone. She felt it was her duty to keep him company. He also played on her good heart by calling her and seeking for sympathy whenever he is ill.

My daughter returned home and gradually began to understand for herself just the kind of man Simon really was. She spoke to him every now and then and visited him every now and then if she wanted to. Simon had lost any respect she had ever had for him.

It is now 16 years since I left Simon and he is still alone while I have been remarried to a loving man. I have had at least two of Simon's girlfriends over the years complain about his behaviour to me. Simon hardly calls me now, but texts whenever he feels like it to release some of his BS, but I am not bothered. Since I began using spiritual healing techniques towards him he rarely contacts the children or me. The spiritual healing technique can be found in the ebook "Surviving Domestic Violence Info & Tips" on www. survivingdomesticviolence.info

The boys stopped seeing or speaking with him about two or three years ago. I believe he would not recognise them if he met them on the street. All the children have decided of their own accord not to have Simon in their lives. They are more focused on their lives and in forming a happier relationship with my husband, who loves them, is there for them and cares for them more than Simon ever did.

And we live on.

A wise man adapts himself to circumstances as water shapes itself to the vessel that contains it.

– Chinese Proverb

CHAPTER LESSONS

Abuser's Controlling Tactics

1. Distressing the children.

2. Attempt to destroy the children's confidence in me - their mother.

My Strategies

1. Took year out to rest and spend with children.

2. Got children involved in decision making; especially when they've been promised attention.

3. Took time to study abuser's motivation.

4. Conquered domestic violence by forgiving abuser, forgiving myself for letting it happen to me, letting go, and moving on completely.

5. Put it out there – requested EXACTLY the type of man I wanted to marry and the kind of relationship I wanted while being the type of woman for that type of man.

Could Have Done & Recommendations

1. Get professional help for the children to cope with the abuser's distress and disruptions.

2. Find ways to prevent my daughter going to spend time with him and preventing the abuser abusing her.

Conclusion

If you have experienced domestic violence, you may relate to some of my experiences mentioned in this book.

If you have not experienced it then you are now aware of what it is and what to look out for. I pray it does not happen to you.

If you know someone who has mentioned any signs of abuse to you and they don't know it is part of domestic violence, direct them to read this book for them to know and get help and also to download the FREE ebook on "Surviving domestic violence Info & Tips" on www.survivingdomesticviolence.info

My experience of this adversity – domestic violence, has given me a new angle in life especially about relationships. With any adversity you may experience, be it with relationship or something else I want you to know that you can overcome it and excel in life no matter what and remember that the situation is only temporary. You also have to remember that your life is in your hands and you can change things around for the better and so be in charge by making the right choices and taking right decisions. It may be hard for you while in it to have the strength to think right, but remember if I can do it, so can you. You have my story as reference and I urge you to learn from my mistakes and from my courage.

From my experience of domestic violence and the experiences of many women I have come across and helped; I have found that domestic violence is the same all over the world. Domestic violence is not a respecter of race, age, culture, demographic location, position or status.

Men who are violent do so out of insecurity. They are insecure and feel the only way to be in control is to exert their power over someone else and they feel that will help them to feel secure and respected. This is wrong, wrong and so wrong. It isn't right on any level but to them it does feel right. I believe most of them do not know otherwise and find it hard to accept they are insecure and seek to be in control.

From what I know now, it is true that people can only act accordingly to their level of thinking, knowledge and understanding. There is a high need for more education on self-esteem, self-confidence and self-love. Men have to learn that to be in control they don't have to exert their power over anyone, especially women to stop them feeling insecure. With their self-esteem, self-confidence and self-love in place, they will find that that's all they need to gain respect because they will be in control of their own lives.

Now as a Life Coach and Transformational Speaker working with women, empowering and inspiring them, what I'll say is this; **I suffered this, so you don't have to.** I have trainings; workshops and coaching programs specifically meant for women only who have experienced domestic violence to help them in gaining back their self-esteem and self-confidence and for those who need help with taking charge of their lives. If you are one of those or know anyone in this situation, I can help you or them. All you have to do is visit. www.felicityokolo.com on Training page to enroll or email felicity@felicityokolo.com and request for details.

Courage is not the absence of fear, but rather the judgment that something else is more important than fear.

– Ambrose Redmoon

My Take on Domestic Violence

Domestic violence is like a plague. People see it and disregard it. Some try to disinfect it using disinfectant wipes. That is not the solution. You don't eradicate a plague by using disinfectant wipes.

* * *

Domestic violence seems to be on the rise. There is an increase in shelters for victims. Support groups for victims and families keep forming. There is an increase in perpetrator arrests and perpetrator programmes. Why is this so? The government and everyone else seem to be tackling domestic violence from the effects point. They seem to be treating the symptoms rather than the cause.

While some of the programs work, the main focus of the government and other agencies really has to be on the victims and victims-to-be. They are the ones who can help to eradicate this plague. To eradicate this plague we must all see domestic violence as a global problem. We must all learn what it is and be aware of it. If it does not affect you directly it definitely affects you indirectly through a family member, friend, neighbour, or colleague. If a colleague from work was abused and doesn't show up for work because she has been beaten, you end up doing their work. If you are an employer and your employee was beaten and doesn't show up for work, you are left to get a replacement worker, do her work yourself or do without. If you are trying to have a good night sleep and your neighbour is screaming in pain because she is being beaten, how can you get that good night sleep? If you know your friend or relative is being abused, you are concerned for their safety! Do you now see how we all are affected by domestic violence directly or indirectly? If ignored, the energy of domestic violence on the victims around you floats about and sticks onto you - even though you turned a blind eye. You are drowning in that sad energy. Yet, you pretend it is not there.

When a victim or survivor tells people who have not experienced domestic violence about their experience it usually renders others speechless. They do not know what to say. Their body language changes instantly, their voice tone changes and they quickly go into sympathy mode or shock. Some become apologetic and others become con-fused. They look as if they just want to leave or get away from hearing more about your experiences. All of a sudden you are a different person. You start to feel isolated again, which is what you were trying to prevent in the first place. These reactions are the very reason why you were reluctant to tell people your experience in the first place. You begin to feel like they are judging you or that their sympathy is false. You start worrying why they are apologetic or sympathetic.

It is important to tell your story and to get it off your chest to make people aware of domestic abuse and its effects on peoples' lives. All you want to do is let them know you better and you want them to understand why you do the things you do. All you want is to be 'normal' and accepted as 'normal'; without making people feel uncomfortable or upset.

Some people are quick to start thinking of how to help you without understanding what you want or why you are telling them. Some close friends or family members are very upset and want to avenge for you or beat up the perpetrator. You don't stop violence with violence. While all these people have good intentions they are going about it the wrong way. For more information on how you can help victims of domestic violence visit: **www.felicityokolo.com/blog**, and also available in the ebook on surviving domestic violence.

Everybody needs to be aware of domestic violence and how it affects us globally and its cost on our lives, the government, etc. Everyone needs to know that we have to tackle and eradicate this plague together. For that to become reality, resources need to target the root cause of domestic violence. Why not prevent instead of pouring and wasting funds on more arrests, more refuge for victims and their families, more domestic violence courts, etc.? While these are necessary, they don't eradicate; they only treat the symptoms of domestic violence.

Resources must be focused and targeted on the root cause of domestic violence. By doing so you are sure to eradicate the plague. Resources are needed to train potential victims-to-be about domestic violence before they become victims. This also holds true with individuals who have experienced domestic violence. It needs to stop with them and not trickle down to the future generations.

By training girls from age 12 about domestic violence and its effects and on self-esteem, self-love, self-confidence and what a healthy relationship should be, there is a likelihood that domestic violence cases will stop increasing, will hopefully result in more arrests and less acceptance by frightened victims.

Victims of domestic violence are getting younger and this training will teach them how to spot abusive partners and prevent the urge to conform and accept or tolerate domestic violence. This will save young women from being victims. For more information on training on self-esteem and self-confidence for girls, victims and survivors visit:

www.felicityokolo.com on Training page
Or send an email to: felicity@felicityokolo.com.

Training for victims will help them make right decisions in regards to the effects of domestic violence on them. They don't always see them at first, although almost everybody else does.

For survivors, the training will help them rebuild their lives by first helping reinstate their self-esteem, self-love and self-confidence. It will help them overcome and conquer; while teaching them how to prevent domestic violence in future relationships. This can make the difference for future generations and on how to raise their children on living a life free from violence.

Children of victims and survivors who have witnessed or experienced domestic violence need to be counselled and trained as well. They do not have to carry the pain with them or become violent because of their anger. If everyone in all categories mentioned above are aware and realise what to do, it will make a huge difference. The energy you absorb from this plague does not have to remain with you and you can stop it from crippling the world.

According to statistics by Women's Aid Charity in the UK, **one in four women** will be a victim of domestic violence in their lifetime – many of these women get abused on a number of occasions. On average, **two women a week** are killed by a current or former male partner in the **UK**. In the United States, one in four women will experience domestic violence in their lifetime according to National Coalition Against Domestic Violence (NCADV). Also according to the U.S. Department of Justice's National Crime Victimization Survey (NCVS), a domestic violence act occurs every 15 seconds in the United States resulting in about 2.5 million women experiencing domestic violence each year. On average **three women are killed every day in the U.S** due to domestic violence according to The National Organisation for Women.

For more information on surviving domestic visit: www.survivingdomesticviolence.info to download surviving domestic violence info & Tips booklet or email: felicity@felicityokolo.com and I will send you a download of the booklet.

There are three things victims can do to help decrease domestic violence and even eliminate it and they are:

1. Preventing/Avoiding it.
2. Don't tolerate it.
3. Post domestic violence therapy & training for the victims and their families.

Preventing/Avoiding Domestic Violence

Women have to be aware of what domestic violence is. Again here is a definition; domestic violence – also called domestic abuse, battering or intimate partner violence – *"is a pattern of controlling and aggressive behaviours from one adult towards another within the context of an intimate relationship."* The abuse can be physical, verbal, sexual, mental, emotional, financial and social isolation. All these abuse comes from the abuser's desire for **power and control.** For detailed list of the various forms of abuse visit www.survivingdomesticviolence.info to download surviving domestic violence info and tips booklet or email: felicity@felicityokolo.com and I will send you a download of the booklet.

If you are dating a man and see any of the common abusive behaviours or tendencies, take them as serious warning signs of domestic violence. If you see those signs while dating him; imagine what it will be like when you live together. The more time you spend with someone, the more hidden characteristics about him or her you begin to see. In some cases you may not see those warning behaviours. This is either because the marriage is forced or arranged, you did not date long enough, or you had long distance dating.

In some cases, if there is violence in a home, men from such homes will become violent towards their partners. This particularly holds true if the mother stayed with their abuser. It would save a lot of pain for you to discuss your concerns about domestic violence with your partner when you start dating and watch their reactions. Also ask for their views on the matter. Tell them your fears and concerns. Be firm while doing it with love.

Find out about your partners' family background and find out if there was violence in his family. Also share your 'ideal' happy loving relationship and dreams with your partner. Let him share his with you as well. This will help you see what both of you have in common. If you don't have an 'ideal' here are some examples of values you may want: freedom, love, respect, honesty, peace, happiness (more of these most of the time is ideal). Point out to them what constitutes abusive behaviours and make it clear to him that you will not tolerate it. Also it would not be right neither will it create a happy environment to live in; much less raise a family in. If you are happy then proceed, if you are not happy with their views and reactions regarding domestic violence; retreat. It is a very good way to lay down your ground rules upfront. This has worked for me and other women to prevent domestic violence in our relationships. Apart from deterring your spouse, the fact that it is what you want and believe in also increases your chances of attracting the right loving non-violent partner.

Don't Tolerate Domestic Violence

If a man abuses you once, the probability of him doing it again is very, very high. You might dismiss it as a mistake or try and come up with some creative reason or excuse for him. That is justifying and it does not change how high the probability of him hitting again is. He might come up with very creative reasons or excuses such as he was drunk, upset, stressed, under pressure, you made him do it, etc. He may be so apologetic that he kneels down, cries and lavishes you with presents. Those things last as long as a flower out of water. Believe me, I have seen it, others have and your situation will most likely not be any different.

Most of the time the abuse starts with name-calling and other non-physical abusive behaviours as listed out in the ebook mentioned above. It then progresses to physical. Treat both non-physical and physical as the same. I have seen women who have never experienced physical abuse, but have suffered and been seriously damaged by non-physical abuse.

If you start experiencing the abuse, it is your time to either find a way **to stop it or leave.** For me there are only two options: the violence has to stop or you leave - unless you want to be seriously damaged or pay the price and be killed. The choice, however, is yours. I strongly believe in these two options because there is no other one that will let you survive.

A way to stop the abuse will be by having discussions with your partner and not letting the line continue to be crossed. Also, both of you could attend marriage counselling and you can get similar marriage or relationship help that is available in your area by searching online or through Citizens Advice Bureau. Your partner could also attend a program called Help for Perpetrator or similar help programmes available as mentioned above in the ebook. You could also try some spiritual ways such as praying, ho'oponopono or any other thing both of you can come up with. You may also want to do a combination of any of the above mentioned.

The main focus is for the abuse to stop. It does not matter which way that is achieved so long as the abuse stops. You may be able to influence change in his behaviour, especially with spiritual methods, but I must warn you that a lot of men who believe in controlling their partner may not see their behaviour as wrong and will not see the importance of attending marriage counselling or a perpetrator program. They might even become angry with you for thinking they have a problem or that the marriage they view as perfect is not viewed that way by you. They might even become violent at your suggestion for them to get help, so be mindful of how you approach this. I also recommend you try and stop the abuse using methods most appropriate for you before leaving, if you want to. That way you know deep in your heart you have tried all you can to make the relationship work. Do not leave it too long or you might be sorry you did.

Leaving is your other option. It shows that you will not tolerate abuse. Leaving does a lot for you. From my experience and those of other women, leaving is the last resort after trying many things to make the relationship work. I kicked myself for not leaving after the first physical abuse from Simon. That decision to stay and try again almost cost me my life – either Simon killing me or me taking my own life. Either way I would have been dead. Like many women I kept thinking things would get better, he would change, it was for the sake of the children and countless other stupid excuses that get called reasons.

Leaving is probably the most courageous thing you can do as a woman experiencing domestic violence. It's courageous because you are stepping into the unknown (except the fact that you will be alive). Please note that a lot of women are killed within few months of leaving their abuser. The abuser feels he has lost control and wants to kill you if he cannot control you. I will suggest you be on your guard and stay safe at least a year after leaving the abuser. Avoid meeting the abuser one-to-one in isolated places or avoid face-to-face contact with him totally if you can help it. Leaving is also courageous because you will be worried about supporting yourself and your children, if you have any. You have the worry about the stigma over your family, worry about your culture, your religion, starting all over again, how people will view you and what they will say. You and your children don't need to become a community statistic. You don't need to feel shame when you tell people what you have been through.

For me, I see violence as something bad and wrong. I do not feel ashamed of telling people what happened to me. The more ashamed women are of telling their stories or speaking out about domestic violence the worse it gets. The abuser feels they can keep abusing you because you feel ashamed of telling people and they continue to get away with it. There is no shame in speaking about it. In fact, the more you speak about it the easier it is for the shame to transfer onto the abuser, if at all he feels any shame.

You must not suffer both ways: as the victim and the shamed. One way is bad enough. It is not right or empowering for you to remain in the victim mode and wait for the world to take care of you and feel sorry for you for the rest of your life. Leaving shows your statement that you deserve better, that you know what you want for yourself in your life and what you want out of life. Leaving shows you want to be in charge of your life and the results in it. Also if the results you are getting are not what you want, then you have the power to change them because you will be in charge.

As for stigma on family, like I told my parents *if you want to marry Simon be my guest.* I wore the shoes and knew where it hurt; not them. If they didn't want to be my parents anymore that is fine. They should remember who abandoned whom. Besides, I was divinely given friends who acted like parents to me when I needed parents. I believe if you are in a similar situation, one where your family members are threatening to abandon you unless you do what you don't want to do, my recommendation is to go with your heart and do what you want to do because all you need will be given to you. Most of the time, your family do eventually come around.

Fear of Cultural/Traditional Or Religious Beliefs

A lot of women are afraid of leaving because of cultural or religious beliefs. For both cultural and religious beliefs I have a simple take; any religion or culture/tradition that supports or promotes abuse of a person should be scrapped. As an Ibo woman my culture/tradition does not support abuse of women contrary to 'normal' understanding of some people. It was just a cover-up that men use to hold women down. Women themselves have long held themselves down too by believing that to be a successful woman you have to be married or have a man around even if you were being treated badly. For me that is a truckload of B.S. I believe similar thing happen in other cultures/tradition where women are repressed. I am pleased that women are slowly moving away from such beliefs that hold them down.

Humans made traditions and most were made so long ago that they need reviewing. These traditions can be changed by humans to fairer ones for today's modern world. Most people who are against review of traditions are usually those who enjoy seeing people suffer and it all stems from control, instead of love.

Fear Of The Unknown

Many women don't leave because they are afraid of the unknown. I love the unknown. Why? I love the unknown because I can make it into what I want it to be. The unknown does not exist as far as I'm concerned, so why fear what does not exist? Your fear of the unknown stems from your past or present experiences that you use to predict your future. That leads to scaring yourself.

See the unknown as just what it is without reference to your past and present. Since it is unknown you can be in the know of what it will be by creating it just as you want. Focus on what you want ONLY. Be persistent, be firm and do what's necessary to make it what you want. If you worry you are bringing in fear that will cripple you. F.E.A.R (False Evidence Appearing Real) as I call and teach it, is all made up. For more information on banishing F.E.A.R. refer to my book "Who Stole My Power? And The Easy Way To Reclaim!" by visiting www.whostolemypower.com. You have experienced abuse and want better for yourself, so go ahead and create it.

As for religious beliefs, many Christians like me believe that the Bible does not approve divorce. Well so do I, but at what cost I ask? The same Bible that does not approve of divorce also teaches, *"Thou shall not kill"*. This means literally killing someone and also includes fighting and abusing someone. For me, I understand that I am not allowed to kill, fight, hurt or abuse someone and neither shall I wait and tolerate someone hurting, abusing and threatening to kill me. If I know my life is in danger and chose to stay and was killed - in other words I have killed myself - I would have broken the commandment *"Thou shall not kill"*. This same commandment applies to the abusers who tend to overlook it as they please. In the same Bible it is written about love in the family and how a man should love his wife like his body.

I think if a man does not love you like his body he is not the right man for you.

I believe the teachings of the Bible are fair and must not be misconstrued and misinterpreted to look like it approves of human suffering. I also believe the commandments and teachings of the Bible are made for humans and not humans for the commandments and teachings.

Domestic Violence & Future Generation

Leaving an abusive relationship also helps prevent domestic violence in future generation. This is true because if you have children who witnessed you being abused repeatedly as they grew up, they are more likely to be involved in abuse themselves – either as the victim or perpetrator. Although you didn't wish that for them, but that is how you indirectly raised them to be. They think and believe that it is the right way to treat someone or to be treated. They might even abuse you too.

Leaving as soon as possible and raising your children away from abusive homes is probably one of the most sure fire ways of preventing domestic violence in future generations. This creates the opportunity for the cycle to break because children not raised in abusive homes are less likely to abuse their partners. Even if they do, they are more likely to get help in resolving their problems. That is often not the case for those who are raised in abusive homes.

Women, if you are staying because of your children, you are probably doing more damage than good to them because they will not respect you or your partner. They will be upset with you for staying in such an environment. They will have anger problems and other emotional and psychological issues; plus an increased chance of taking the violence to the next generation. Not all children will exhibit all the above mentioned things, but most will. Your leaving gives your children a better chance of being happy and successful in life. You also get the chance to create the life you truly want.

Post domestic violence therapy & training for the victims and their families

As a solution based thinker, I like to come up with solutions to problems rather than dwelling on who did what? If you've experienced domestic violence and left your abuser, your first focus will be to get help. Help with basic needs such as housing and finances if you lost those in the process of leaving. Most importantly, get help with your emotional and mental health. Counselling will help you deal with and get rid of the pain, frustration, anger, blame, depression etc. You'll need to talk about your experience openly, without feeling judged or ashamed. You'll need to start acting like a survivor, not as a victim. You were a victim while in the abusive relationship, but after you leave, you are no longer a victim but a survivor. After survivor you move on to being a conqueror.

To me, survivor means you have stepped out of the abusive relationship and know you deserve better. To me, conqueror means you have forgiven your abuser, you have released all petty anger and the negativity you held against the abuser because you are too good and strong to waste your energy on him. When you become a conqueror, you have taken charge of your life. You are as free as the wind to Be, Do and Have whatever you want in life. You would be foolish to let your past hold you back by constantly looking back and casting blame.

You have to take 100% responsibility for your life and the results in it. While you were in the abusive setting you did not take responsibility and you let the abuse happen to you. Yes, you did, I did for a while too. Only you have the power to change your life. Once you've made that decision to change, you might as well do it properly. There are a variety of help and programs available for you to tap into. Ask your local Citizens Advice Bureau or search online. I also have a program specifically designed to help women who have experienced domestic to take charge of their lives and create the life they truly want. This Training is called **"It Is My Life And I'm In Charge".** You can access it by visiting and enrolling at:

www.felicityokolo.com on the Training page

Or emailing:

felicity@felicityokolo.com.

You must set goals for yourself and lay ground rules, especially for your future relationships. You need to make sure you prevent domestic violence as how it is mentioned in preventing domestic violence section above. It is best to raise your children in a loving happy home. Teach them how to love and other non-violent ways to resolve conflict or problems. This is crucial in helping them change. They've witnessed terrible things while you were suffering abuse. You must teach them that domestic violence or any form of violence is bad and wrong. It is not acceptable and that was why you left. Setting boundaries and teaching your children the right way to resolve conflict and the effects of domestic violence on people helps break the cycle of domestic violence.

Winners Or Losers?

No one wins in domestic violence. Everyone loses: you, the abuser, the children, your extended families, the community, the government and non-governmental agencies. Every person is affected.

Domestic violence is a global issue. You must play your role to prevent and end domestic violence by using any of the methods mentioned above if you are in abusive situation right now. If you don't, you are not playing your role to end this global problem and you are therefore indirectly condoning it and allowing it to cripple the world.

At a conference on women leadership there was a panel that spoke about women as being very powerful and the various roles of women in the world. Some others spoke of domestic violence, rape and other abuse girls and women experience across the world. I found both messages conflicting and asked the panel what were a comment and a question combined. I asked, "If women are truly powerful as mentioned and they are leaders with power to change and influence, why do we hear women being abused and raped by men that they raised? What is going on? Where is that power that is talked about? Could it be that women are not playing their roles properly?"

I got two answers; the first speaker talked about the failure of women to carry on raising boys during the teenage stage in their lives. She went on to say that if women believed their role as mothers ended once boys became teenagers they would lose control of the boys. The result would be they would likely grow up to be influenced by their peers or act without direction. The second speaker answered by saying that those boys have a mind of their own and no matter how the women raised them they would still turn out how they wanted and most were influenced by their peers or bad companies.

I would like to add to the panels' answers by firstly saying that both speakers made valid points. I believe women are very powerful. Women hold the key to making this world free of domestic violence and sexual violence by using their power of change and influence. If a woman uses her power of change and influence, it becomes a blessing. If she fails to use it, the power becomes a curse. That power to change and influence must be used in preventing domestic violence and not tolerating it. Teach children a non-violent way of resolving conflict. That is how you raise children to be happy and loving children from childhood to 21. By doing that, men also learn to respect and love women. They don't just see them as sex slaves or the weaker sex for them to repress.

When you, as a woman, recognise that you have the key to ending domestic violence by reporting it and not tolerating it, that will help put an end to the vicious cycle of abuse.

When you start taking 100% responsibility for your life and the role you play in the world you can start making a massive change in the world - starting from your home. That is how domestic violence incidents start decreasing. Then people will start listening to you and you will gain the respect you so highly deserve from men and the world as a whole. You may not have gotten it before, but that will change. You will have the opportunity to influence changes to policies that you have been fighting for for years. That is how you can get men to accept your opinions and listen to you. That is when it will happen - you will be the master of your life.

By first pointing the finger to yourself and fixing yourself, you will find that all other things will begin to fall into place. Then and only then will you be in control and exercise your power as a woman to shape the world and be in charge of your life while you are doing it.

XOXO

Sometimes adversity is what you need to face in order to become successful.

– Zig Ziglar

Goal Setting Audio CD

In this goal setting audio recorded live over the phone with you will learn the following:

• Reasons why people don't set goals.

- Why setting goal is important if you want to be successful.

- Some best strategies to use to set goals so you stay focused and motivated all the way!

- The key strategies for writing goals

- The Magic Formula to achieving your goals

- The Right Mindset needed to achieve your goals.

- How your BRAIN and SUBCONSCIOUS mind works to support you

- Tips and many many more...   **£14.99**

Who Stole My Power? And The Easy Way To Reclaim It!
– AUDIO CD   **£16.99**

It Is My Life And I'm In Charge
– AUDIO CD   **£19.99**

Surviving Domestic Violence Info & Tips Booklet (A6 Print Version)

Surviving Domestic Violence Info & Tips Booklet (Free Download)

Visit: www.survivingdomesgticviolence.info

Email: info@felicityokolo.com for bulk purchase only

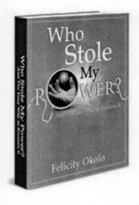

Who stole my power? And The Easy Way To Reclaim It!

Living Your Ideal Life Doesn't Have To Be Hard!

This book is about we as super-beings playing small. The book shows you how to start using your power as a god to excel in life. If your power as a god has been stolen, it shows you how to reclaim it and live loving, joyful life to your true potential while enabling others to do the same.

Too many of us live our lives in worry of fulfilling our material desires and fear of the unknown. We tend to search for directions in all the wrong places and before you realise it, your power to excel in life is stolen.

In this book you'll learn:

- How to banish fear of the unknown and limiting beliefs
- How to overcome being overwhelmed & gain balance in your life
- How to gain clarity for direction by asking empowering questions
- How to tap into your infinite power of imagination & intuition

£9.99

COACHING PROGRAMS

Who Stole My Power?
And The Easy Way To Reclaim It!

A Coaching program designed to help you find your source of power and show you how to maximise it effectively. If you have lost your power, we show you how to reclaim it and equally excel in life.

Duration: 6 months – 12 months

It Is My Life And I'm In Charge (women only)

A Coaching Program specially designed for women who have experienced domestic violence. This program focuses on helping women reconnect with their higher purpose to create the life they truly want.

Duration: 6 months – 12 months

TRAINING PROGRAMS

Who Stole My Power? And The Easy Way To Reclaim It! - Workshop

A one-day workshop focused on helping people gain clarity and purpose in their lives.

ONE-DAY WORKSHOP

Who Stole My Power? And The Easy Way To Reclaim It!

CITE FEMME LTD
Life is good. Life is Effortless

20% DISCOUNT

- One coupon per person
- One coupon per workshop/program and not to be used in conjunction with other promotions.

Signed: Felicity Okolo

WSMP01

It Is My Life And I'm In Charge - Workshop (Women Only)

A one-day workshop focused on helping women who have experienced domestic violence start regaining charge of their lives.

ONE-DAY WORKSHOP

It Is My Life And I'm In Charge – Workshop (Women Only)

CITE FEMME LTD
Life is good. Life is Effortless

20% DISCOUNT
- One coupon per person
- One coupon per workshop/program and not to be used in conjunction with other promotions.

Signed: Felicity Okolo

IIML01

Train - A -Trainer Program

A program focused on training people on our various trainings and workshops.

TRAINING

Train - A -Trainer Program

CITE FEMME LTD
Life is good. Life is Effortless

20% DISCOUNT
- One coupon per person
- One coupon per workshop/program and not to be used in conjunction with other promotions.

Signed: Felicity Okolo

TATP01

Self-Esteem & Self-Confidence Training

Training designed to teach people how to develop their self-esteem and self-confidence enabling them to reach their true potential.

TRAINING

Self-Esteem & Self-Confidence Training

CITE FEMME LTD
Life is good. Life is Effortless

20% DISCOUNT
- One coupon per person
- One coupon per workshop/program and not to be used in conjunction with other promotions.

Signed: Felicity Okolo

SESC01

Women Empowerment Training

A one-day workshop empowering women on 3 human desires of Love, Health and Wealth to reveal and put in place the necessary strategies for each woman to apply in their live.

ONE-DAY WORKSHOP

Women Empowerment Training

CITE FEMME LTD
Life is good. Life is Effortless

20% DISCOUNT
- One coupon per person
- One coupon per workshop/program and not to be used in conjunction with other promotions.

Signed: Felicity Okolo

WET01

Wealth Creation

A one-day introductory workshop on wealth creation strategies. This will help you figure out the best channels and strategies to start creating your wealth. If you are already on your way, the course will help put better strategies in place and help you stay focused.

ONE-DAY WORKSHOP

Wealth Creation

CITE FEMME LTD
Life is good. Life is Effortless

20% DISCOUNT
- One coupon per person
- One coupon per workshop/program and not to be used in conjunction with other promotions.

Signed: Felicity Okolo

WE01

Public Speaking

A one-day introductory workshop to public speaking. This will introduce you to key skills necessary to be an effective speaker and communicator while boosting your confidence levels.

ONE-DAY WORKSHOP

Public Speaking

CITE FEMME LTD
Life is good. Life is Effortless

20% DISCOUNT
- One coupon per person
- One coupon per workshop/program and not to be used in conjunction with other promotions.

Signed: Felicity Okolo

PS01

About The Author

Felicity Okolo is one of the UK's leading experts in the development of human potential. She is a Life Coach, a dynamic, transformational and entertaining speaker and trainer.

She has a wonderful ability to inform, influence and inspire audiences towards increased levels of self-esteem, to create a more powerful and purposeful future for themselves while taking personal responsibility for their lives.

She is the author and narrator of the books; *Who Stole My Power? And The Easy Way To Reclaim It!* AND *It Is My Life And I'm In Charge.*

Felicity is a regularly featured speaker for government and non-government organisations, churches and corporations.

Felicity works with people (individuals and organisations) especially women on personal empowerment and development. She runs a series of coaching programs, workshops and trainings.

Felicity's purpose in life is to *Empower and lead people in a dynamic and passionate manner to live to their true potential, all happy, healthy and prosperous, expressing love and peace for the highest good of all concerned.*

For further information about Felicity and her coaching programs, workshops and trainings email: felicity@felicity-okolo.com or visit www.felicityokolo.com.

Lightning Source UK Ltd.
Milton Keynes UK
UKOW050247240412

191337UK00001B/5/P